TEACHING HARD
TEACHING SOFT

A Structured Approach to Planning
and Running Effective Training Courses

Teaching . . . . that is
helping people to learn

You'll soon get the
hang of it: Video Arts

TEACHING HARD TEACHING SOFT

A Structured Approach to Planning and Running Effective Training Courses

Colin Corder

Illustrations by Pete Boggon

Gower

Published by
Gower Publishing Company Limited
Gower House
Croft Road
Aldershot
Hants   GU11 3HR
England

Gower Publishing Company
Old Post Road
Brookfield
Vermont 05036
USA

Reprinted 1991

British Library Cataloguing in Publication Data
Corder, Colin
    Teaching hard, Teaching soft.
    1. Personnel
    I. Title
    658.3124

Library of Congress Cataloging-in-Publication Data
Corder, Colin, 1941–
    Teaching hard, teaching soft / Colin Corder.
        p.   cm.
    Includes bibliographical references.
    Includes index.
    1. Employee training directors—Training of.   2. Employees-
-Training of.   3. Teaching.   I. Title.
HF5549.5.T7C597   1990
658.3′12404—dc20   90-37470
                                                          CIP

ISBN 0 566 02865 4

Printed in Great Britain by Galliard (Printers) Ltd, Great Yarmouth

Contents

Contents

Figures

Preface

Those who can, do; those who can't, teach . . .

George Bernard Shaw's aphorism was once applied to me by a manager who was less than enthralled with my performance as a systems analyst. I had completed a year's posting overseas and the company was contractually bound to find a job for me on completion of the tour. My manager had to make a recommendation as to where I could usefully be employed. Bereft of inspiration as to where to locate such a deadbeat he recommended that I join the training division.

Shaw's dictum is widely quoted and generally regarded as embodying at least a part truth. In reality the implication contained in it is wholly and disastrously wrong. A good systems analyst can affect the design of one system every three years; a good manager's influence is extended through his subordinates. But as a teacher, if I can teach good systems analysis or effective management, then I influence countless systems and many management situations. The logical conclusion of this is that the training department should not be a penal colony for failed practitioners but the place where the organization's brightest talents are deployed.

The inspiration for this book came when I was reading through the evaluations of a series of two-day communication courses I had given in Australia. A delegate had written the following comment: 'I thought the first day was almost totally useless. In fact I nearly did not come back for the second. I'm only glad that I did. It was exactly what I came to learn.'

The evaluation form specifically invites participants to say what they liked best and least about the course. The above remark was the most extreme statement of a pattern of clear preferences for the second of the two days. What then was different about the second day? The participants were the same, the lecturer was the same. Both days had an equal amount of participation. There had been no other relevant changes. The only variable was the material; people preferred the content of the second day to that of the first.

So what was the difference? To me the first day had the more important teaching points — targeting your audience, knowing your material and being clear about the objectives of a communication. Getting the structure right. These are the main issues that people get wrong in any form of communication. The second day was more detailed. It contained specific rules for writing, tips for drawing visuals, checklists for presentations. Most of this could equally well have been found in the right books. But this was what my audience had come for. It was their reaction that alerted me to the distinction between teaching 'soft' concepts and 'hard' facts. Ultimately it gave rise to this book.

A book, like a course, needs a specification. This book is aimed primarily at people involved in business training (although I believe strongly that the theory propounded has relevance to all teaching situations). It is about the specification, design, writing and presentation of a training programme or course. It has objectives at various levels. The title is derived from my division of subjects — and approaches to teaching — into 'hard' and 'soft'. This is the theory which I have attempted to apply to all aspects of the trainer's job. My experience, from training trainers, is that experienced trainers will find that this clarifies many common decisions and problems and provides a view and notation that is particularly relevant to specifying and designing courses. In following this theme through, I have attempted to devise rules, where applicable, guidelines where not, to help course designers, writers and presenters. Finally, there are sundry tricks of the trade which may throw light on specific areas and help put together a more effective learning activity.

The switch in terminology from 'training' to 'learning' gives me the opportunity to clarify some usages in the book. The word 'teaching' has connotations of the school classroom. It runs counter to modern theory, which emphasizes 'learning'. In many ways this is a healthy swing of the pendulum away from the Victorian style of cramming facts into reluctant pupils. But pendulums have a habit of swinging too far before a sensible equilibrium is reached. Discovery and experiential learning are fashionable concepts. As if all we need to do is to create a learning situation and let the students take it from there. But we are still teaching. Even if we are teaching people to question things rather than to learn by rote, we still need to be clear about the type of questions we think they should ask. This book is therefore directed at teachers, whether they call themselves trainers, instructors, lecturers or presenters. I use all these terms, purely for variation; as far as this book goes, they are synonymous. The same applies to those at the receiving end, who are variously referred to as students, participants, trainees and delegates.

The use of the words 'training' and 'education' is another fertile source of confusion. In some usages (as in 'I work for a training company') education is a subset of training; in others ('the Department of Education and Science') training is a subset of education. The usage of these words will be more closely examined in Chapter 4.

The same problem arises with the desire to use non-sexist language.

'Men' — and its pronoun derivatives — is in common use to denote at once a set distinct from women and a superset containing both itself and women. Any author who has struggled to use 'he/she', or even 'their', is trading off felicity of style against accusations of sexism. I shall follow the Interpretation Act 1978 whereby the masculine gender is used in its 'superset' meaning as referring to persons of either sex.

My acknowledgements for this book should embrace the many trainers who in attending my courses have criticized many points, argued others, corroborated yet more. In reading the book, they will see the contribution they have made. If I single out some of my former colleagues in Keith London Associates — Grahame Stehle, Geoff Quentin, Roger Smith, Jim Borritt, Dave Beaumont, Daniel Freedman, Marion Wells — it is because they have specifically contributed either in the development of the course on which this book is based, or in reading and constructively criticizing this text.

Colin Corder

"Mr. O'Neill, in the Oxford School of Philosophy we do not come to conclusions; we examine arguments."

An engineering graduate was taking a second degree in philosophy. His first essay was on utilitarianism — the theory that actions are good to the extent that they maximize human happiness. The essay was politely dissected by his tutor. At the end of the tutorial the engineer professed himself stimulated and impressed by the rigorous logic that had been applied in the destruction of his efforts. 'The only question I have,' he commented picking up his books, 'is what conclusions have we come to?' The tutor took a sip of his sherry: 'Mr O'Neill, in the Oxford School of Philosophy we do not come to conclusions; we examine arguments.'

Part I
Specifying the course

I keep six honest serving-men
(They taught me all I knew)
Their names are What and Why and When
And How and Where and Who.
Rudyard Kipling, Just-So Stories

Kipling's stanza has become a cliché. But sayings become clichés only if they embody some widely-accepted truth. And in specifying training courses one invariably returns to the questions that Kipling's serving-men pose.

Teaching consists first of deciding *what* you are teaching, to *whom*, and *why* they need to learn it. The right time and place — *when* and *where* — does not guarantee success but getting them wrong makes failure more likely. *How* takes up the larger part of this book, but is only in the most general terms part of the specification process.

A large proportion of teaching failures are failures of specification. We devote insufficient thought to the material, the audience and the teaching environment. For this reason the first part of this book is concerned with getting the specification right. There is no point in delivering a riveting message, with lucidity and humour, at the wrong level or to the wrong people. Only when we have got the specification right should we worry about how to implement it.

1

What are we teaching?

At school my best subject was English literature. Once I came top in an exam with a mark of over 70 per cent. What irked me was that my closest friend's best subject was mathematics. When he came top it was with a mark in the high nineties and on one occasion he achieved a mark of 100 per cent.

I doubt whether anyone, anywhere, has ever been awarded 100 per cent in a literature exam. It is not that sort of subject. In geometry there is no argument over the length of the hypotenuse in a given right-angled triangle (if there is it is pretty one-sided). There is one, and one only, correct answer. If someone gets it wrong there are two reasons why this could be. Either the theorem has not been understood, or it has been understood but an error has been made in the calculation. Only the most awkward of pupils will take issue with Pythagoras. But in literature there is no formal proof that Shakespeare was a better playwright than his little-known contemporary, Will Bloggspeare. An opinion poll will not help; most people prefer Barbara Cartland. The only test available appears to be the test of time.

The difference between subjects such as mathematics and literature is enshrined in the academic distinction between science and the arts. A similar distinction is to be found in systems theory. Here the terms 'hard' and 'soft' systems are used. 'Hard' systems are those that obey rigid rules such as the law of conservation of matter. 'Soft' systems are those where no similar rules exist, typically because they are concerned with people rather than machines. 'Hard' systems exhibit a high degree of similarity the world over; 'soft' systems, such as tax or voting systems, manifest a high degree of dissimilarity.

It is possible that a given discipline may be thought of as 'soft' because no one has yet succeeded in discovering or formulating the 'hard' rules that govern it; or the rules are too complex for us to master in their totality. Chess is a 'hard' game played in accordance with strictly-defined rules. This is why computers make good chess players. In theory, given sufficient computing power to analyse all possible lines of continuation, the computer would be unbeatable.* Because the permutations of moves run into many millions the human chess player has to think in a different mode. He thinks strategically. He reduces the near-infinite number of possible positions into guidelines about control of the centre, open files and so on. In so doing he makes transferable the skill the expert has acquired; the subject becomes teachable.

Let us extend the comparison between arts and science and hard and soft.** Mathematics and chemistry are hard subjects. Students are not invited to have an opinion about calculus; they learn it. With unfailing consistency, litmus paper turns red in the presence of an acid. Philosophy, on the other hand, is taught as a soft subject. No one agrees on the answers so teaching concentrates on what questions to ask and on developing the ability to think analytically.

Poetry appreciation is soft, though here we see a most instructive phenomenon — students are taught to examine rhyme and metre and to look for other literary devices such as assonance and alliteration. These are 'pseudo-hard' ways of teaching the subject. English literature cannot be completely subjective; how could people spend three years reading for a degree in something that is totally a matter of personal preference?

The conclusion I draw is that hard and soft, science and arts, are ends of a continuum rather than exclusive sets. What determines the position of a given subject on the continuum is the degree to which our state of knowledge of the subject is firm and predictive. *The harder our knowledge is, the more we teach answers; the softer it is, the more we teach questions.*

The distinction between that which is black and white, and that which is a point on a continuum is crucial. Things black or white are easy — independent thought is reduced to the choice between alternatives and if in doubt the simplest of binary decision mechanisms should be used — toss a coin. A continuum, on the other hand, forces us to think for ourselves. It demands awkward decisions about where exactly we take our position.

As an illustration of the pervasiveness of the hard/soft continuum, consider religion. At the hard end we have Islam, full of rules that closely, and to a high level of detail, dictate right behaviour. The rules are prescriptive and unchallengeable. The reason for this is simple but fundamental — they are perceived as coming from a divine source. The minute you start questioning such rules, or their interpretation, you open up Pandora's Box. At the other end is humanism which denies the existence of any such God-given rules and leaves individuals to follow their own conscience. Between the two — reading from hard to soft —

---

*This gives rise to the joke about two computers playing each other. The 'white' computer starts with P-K4. The 'black' computer thinks for a couple of days and then resigns. Given optimum play on the part of his opponent there is no way in which he can win.

**Because the terms hard and soft are used in their stated meaning throughout this book they will now cease to be enclosed in inverted commas. If a subject is 'hard' in the conventional sense, the adjective 'difficult' will be used.

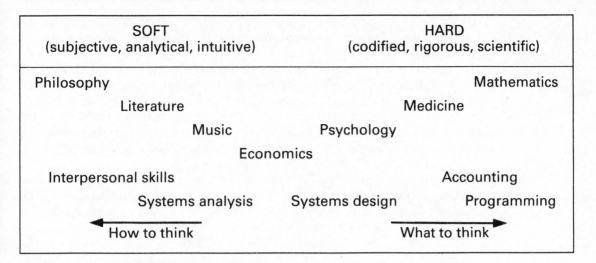

Figure 1.1 The hard/soft continuum

are Catholicism, Protestantism and Quakerism. I leave my readers to place other religions on the scale. But trainers do well to realize that many people — some of them students on courses with no connection to religion — have a hankering for simple, hard, unquestionable truths whether they be embodied in Marxist analysis, belief in the literal truth of the Bible, or the ten commandments of effective selling.

Figure 1.1 maps various subjects on the hard/soft continuum. A wealth of issues is brought out by a diagram like this. One's personal view of a subject is revealed by where one plots it on the continuum. My plotting indicates a reasonably confident view of medicine but less faith in psychology. Economics I put in the middle. The 'law of supply and demand' indicates a hard subject, and it can be taught hard by concentrating on econometrics, but the commonly-held view that six economists will give you seven different opinions makes it sound distinctly soft. In confirmation of this ambivalence, some universities treat it as an arts degree, and others as a science. The same is true of psychology.

Many subjects contain both hard and soft aspects, and which aspect is emphasized may depend on the audience to whom it is being taught. Mathematics is the hardest of subjects to all but mathematicians. At the highest reaches of pure mathematics it becomes extremely soft, to the extent of becoming philosophical. It is no coincidence that many philosophers were also mathematicians. Conversely, although the teaching of philosophy is soft, many philosophers would consider themselves hard. Kant's 'categorical imperative' has a pretty hard ring about it.

History starts by being taught hard at primary school (dates are hard and the binary division into good and bad kings is a classic example of how to impose pseudo-hardness on a soft area). It becomes increasingly soft as you progress through school. The date on which Hitler invaded

5

the Rhineland is specific; whether opposing him would have caused his downfall and thereby avoided the Second World War is a matter of speculation.

Marxism is a failed attempt to convert politics into a hard subject by the discovery of laws which purport to explain the historical necessity of social and economic developments. It is a hard ideology and therefore attracts those who derive intellectual and moral comfort from prescriptive explanations. The similarity often remarked upon between the political extremes of left and right lies in their both being believers in hard truths; it is we moderates who are a soft lot.

English language is hard if grammar is taught; soft, if greater emphasis is placed on creative writing. The complaint of businesspeople that students leave school or university without being able to spell is a call for a move back to teaching English as a hard subject.

Most people are more comfortable with hard teaching than soft for the same reasons that they prefer rule-based moral systems — they like to have things cut and dried, to have their thinking done for them. Decision-making requires analytical thinking, experience and judgement. It is considerably easier as a parent to hand down moral absolutes — *never tell lies* — than to attempt to define the points on the continuum where white lies become grey, and grey become black. At bridge, beginners are taught always to cover an honour with an honour. This is good advice about 95 per cent of the time. The jump from playing by the rule to thinking the situation through for oneself is a big one — in bridge and in life — and one that many people never make.

Research is a conscious attempt to move a subject towards the hard end of the continuum. Scientific discoveries dramatically harden up a subject as what previously was guessed at becomes a law; in intrinsically soft subjects, such as inter-personal skills, we search for 'rules of thumb' or 'guidelines' to impose some measure of formalism and to enable us to teach such intangibles as experience and judgement.

This is not a trivial analysis. Examining a subject for hardness is to put it under a powerful microscope. Essentially it poses the question: 'Given a clear formulation of a problem, will a group of people working independently produce identical solutions?' To take a specific example. How hard an activity is carrying out an audit? The fact that balance sheets balance suggests a rigorous technique — that two accountants, working independently, would finish with the same figures. In that case what is meant by the expression 'creative accounting'? Clearly there is some room for opinion in how one calculates profit and loss. The latter is affected, among other things, by the method and rate of depreciation of assets, valuation of work-in-progress and stock, the provision for bad debts. Notice that as soon as these issues are introduced the accounting course passes from teaching answers, such as net assets = current assets − current liabilities, to teaching questions: 'On what basis should we value stock?'

The analysis of hardness is vital to the person teaching the techniques. To the extent that a subject is hard he is teaching facts and rules and checking students' learning by tests to which there are right answers. To the extent that it is soft he has to make clear that there can be more than one right solution; his job involves the more difficult task of adjudication by comparing the advantages and disadvantages of different solutions or approaches. With hard subjects, students can mark their own work by looking at the answers at the back of the book; in soft subjects only 'model' solutions can be supplied.

It is not sufficient for the teacher to have a view about the relative hardness/softness of what he is teaching. That view must not be far removed from that of the students. If I think of negotiating skills or project leadership as predominantly soft subjects and my students perceive them as hard, then they will come on my course looking for firm rules, when what I am teaching is how to analyse situations with a few 'rules of thumb' thrown in for guidance. In my experience this mismatch is one of the commonest forms of problems in teaching.

Over a number of years I have taken the opportunity afforded by running 'Training the Trainers' courses to ask participants to mark a list of topics out of ten for hardness. The first thing this has done is to validate the terminology since no one has any problem in understanding what is being asked of them. The next thing it does is to bring to light the most interesting divergence of opinion about the topics. The list is:

- Cost-benefit analysis
- Sales presentations
- Problem analysis
- Wine appreciation
- Interviewing
- Principles of financial accounting
- Skiing
- Project leadership
- Spreadsheets
- Social work
- Graphic design
- Report writing

Before proceeding I suggest you attempt this exercise and compare your markings with those of my survey. If there is any topic where you have insufficient knowledge to advance an opinion, just omit it.

Results of hardness survey

Before reading on please recognize that the evaluation is intrinsically soft, in that it tests a matter of opinion. However, the list below is not my personal one. It is a composite of over 300 course participants that have been asked the same question. This itself is a 'hardening up' technique. If your marking were to conflict violently with mine you might, with some legitimacy, argue that it is just a matter of opinion; if it conflicts violently with the average of a survey of 10 000 respondents it begins to look as though it is you who is out of line. Of course you *could* still be right. There are few teachers who have not come across the 'everyone is out of step except me' person on their courses. Once every two centuries such people are proved right! The markings, and my comments, are as follows:

1. *Spreadsheets: 8.9* Not everyone surveyed knows what these are. Those that do mark them high because they are computer-based and pressing a given key always gives the same response. The only soft element is in the use one puts them to rather than in how they work. This difference is explored in the next chapter.

2. *Principles of financial accounting: 8.8* An interesting phenomenon can be seen at work — what I call the 'mystique effect'. People tend to exaggerate the hardness or softness of things they do not understand. As noted above, the fact that a balance sheet balances is prima facie evidence of hardness. But the ability to 'dress' a balance sheet reveals scope for matters of opinion. Nevertheless it takes an accountant — and a cynical one at that — to mark it below 7.

3. *Cost-benefit analysis: 6.7* My students have more faith than I in the objectivity with which the average feasibility study is conducted, viewing it as the scientific collection of a set of data and assumptions and using them to validate a particular course of action. Having undertaken a few in my time, and usually working backwards from the conclusion at which I wish to arrive, I score it considerably lower!

4. *Skiing: 6.5* This is included as an example of a neuro-muscular skill. It typically shows the widest set of marks in any group. The question at issue, explored in the following chapter, is whether the ability to ski depends on an innate ability — a sense of balance — which is not teachable. Those that mark it highly point to rules such as 'always use the edge of your skis'. Those that mark it down are people with two left legs.

5. *Report writing: 5.2* Here we get into the classic argument about the extent to which creative activities can be made rule-based. More of this anon.

6. *Project leadership: 4.6* There is a low standard deviation on this question. Most people appear to agree that leadership is a soft subject. Translated into the wider field of management this is seen in the expression 'Managers are born, not made'. As we shall see, to the extent that this is true we may as well give up on teaching

it. The large number of leadership and management courses indicate that training companies at least think there is something that is teachable.

7. *Sales presentations: 4.4* I once had someone who marked this as 10. I am only pleased he was not on my communications course. Nevertheless, I personally tend to mark it noticeably higher than the average. The same applies to *problem analysis (4.3)* and *interviewing (3.3)*. I teach both these subjects and have therefore spent a lot of time analysing different styles, approaches and so on in order to harden them up.

8. *Graphic design: 3.2* I suffer from the mystique effect with this. I myself am so unartistic that I stand in awe of people who have this ability. It is either innate or so far back in one's early life as to make no difference. I cannot conceive how anyone could ever teach me this subject. However, I observe that styles and fashions come and go. What is good design one year is *passé* the next.

9. *Wine appreciation: 2.8* This average figure conceals a split between the majority of people who rate it soft on the basis that it is all a matter of taste, and the minority who mark it high on the basis that the true expert can accurately tell the region and vintage of a wine in a blind tasting. This difference is expressed in comments of the nature 'It all depends what you mean by wine appreciation'. In this we see how the hard/soft analysis forces people to define the subject matter. This is the basis of all course construction and will be seen throughout this book.

     Personally I mark this topic low on the basis of the expression: 'A glance at the label is worth a lifetime of practice' which seems to indicate a certain lack of confidence in the science, even among its practitioners.

10. *Social work: 2.5* This often brings out the instructive comment: 'There are bits of both'. In as much as social workers must know the relevant legislation, it is hard; in their skill in dealing with people, it is soft.

As we have noted, a comment common to many subjects is that it is a mixture of hard and soft. There is a right answer to where a particular bottle of wine comes from but its quality is more subjective. This distinction between subjects, and within a subject, is crucial. If what we are teaching is hard we have few problems. For someone learning to drive a car, application of the brake pedal will cause the car to slow down. This will happen irrespective of the colour, sex or nationality of the foot applying the pressure. Hard systems are truly non-discriminatory. But the effect of a given action upon the success of negotiations will frequently depend on where the negotiations are being conducted and between whom. The most effective negotiating technique in the USA may be completely counter-productive in the Far East.

Teaching hard subjects calls mainly for in-depth technical knowledge of the subject. The structure of the teaching is a function of the material not the audience. We can apply the term *subject-dependent* to these and draw some provisional conclusions. First, it is easier to teach a hard subject than a soft one; secondly, it is easier to set an examination in a hard subject than a soft one. I would argue that it is for this reason that many degree courses in computing science still devote an inordinate amount of time to truth tables and and/or gates. In fact, the name of the course gives the game away. Taught like this, computing is indeed a science; but the application of computers to everyday business problems remains predominantly an art. This explains why many companies, when recruiting graduates into their computer department, regard a philosophy or English degree as equally relevant as one in computing.

The acid test of subject-dependency is whether a subject can be taught identically the world over. The reverse of this is where a subject is taught differently depending on the circumstances. The question then is 'What are the particular circumstances or variables which make us teach the same subject differently to different people?'

Suppose we are teaching people how to develop business systems. The 'right' design for a production control system depends on the line of business, country in which the company is operating, management style, degree of centralization and a host of other factors. We can categorize these as environmental factors. Their existence means that we cannot teach production control as a hard subject. We can 'harden it up' by finding commonalities — scheduling systems, bill of materials and so on — but essentially we are teaching people to analyse their own environment before applying any general rules. We are teaching the questions that the systems developer has to ask, not the answers that he will impose. We can refer to such subjects as *environment-dependent*.

Some time ago I went to my golf pro for a lesson. Being in a bit of a hurry I interrupted him at one point and said, 'Look, if you'll just describe the correct swing I'll go away and practise it'. I was somewhat crestfallen when he replied, 'There is no such thing as "the correct swing". It's different for everyone. It depends on things like your height, age, whether you're male or female, muscular power and so on.' I tried to fit this into my hard/soft spectrum. Clearly playing golf was not hard. Very early on one was taught some rules about how to grip the club but beyond that people's technique differed widely. Nor was it environment-dependent. How you swing a golf club does not depend on which course you are playing though it can depend on the lie of the ball. My pro's statement was quite clear — different people did it in different ways. The difference was in the person. Suddenly I saw the connection between this statement and what I always say at the start of 'Training the Trainers' courses: 'How people present courses reflects their own personality. Don't think that you necessarily have to be a raging extravert to be a good presenter.'

The third area, therefore, is skills that are *person-dependent*. The most obvious of these are those in which proficiency requires some innate ability such as balance, an eye for a ball or an ear for music. Most of us will never play Chopin's Revolutionary Étude, become scratch golfers or run a four-minute mile no matter how much tuition and practice we have. Though a teacher may bring about some improvement this is likely to depend as much on the student as on the teacher. The really interesting question arises when we substitute acquired personality attributes for the more obvious innate abilities listed above. To what extent is it true when we say that so-and-so will 'never make' a salesman, social worker or teacher? We can look upon this as a reformulation of the nature vs. nurture debate. In posing the question 'Are good managers born or made?' we are asking whether management training is subject-, environment- or person-dependent.* More importantly for us, we are also asking to what extent the skill is teachable.

This approach forces us to think very analytically about the subject we are teaching. Is the material on a course exclusively of one type or a mixture of all three? A course on negotiating skills could include subject-dependent information about the legal side of contracts; it becomes environment-dependent if we recognize the different cultural approaches in different countries to negotiations; and incorporates a person-dependent element if we attempt to develop individuals' own skills by practical work concentrating on their personal strengths and weaknesses.

Postscript:

A good test of a theory is whether it can accommodate examples other than those specifically chosen to illustrate it. I was pleased therefore when a discussion on sentencing policy fitted within the analysis. A baby-batterer had been let off with an extremely lenient sentence. A member of parliament, asked to comment, stated that there should be minimum sentences for such an offence. What she was saying was that sentencing was too soft — too much discretion being allowed based on the offender's circumstances (environment-dependent) or the judge's own views (person-dependent). A minimum sentence, i.e., a hard rule reducing the discretionary element, would make sentencing policy more consistent.

---

*Notice that my point is not that such skills are *totally* person-dependent. We can perhaps identify some subject-dependent elements and certainly some environment-dependent ones. A good wartime leader can be a bad peace-time prime minister. I am reasonably good at teaching businessmen and lousy at teaching my own kids.

2

Why are we teaching?

I studied German for five years at school. My teacher was brilliant. The brighter kids tended to do Latin, but regularly all his pupils passed 'O' level German with marks varying from 60 to 90 per cent. I got 88 per cent. The only problem is — I can't speak German. Rightly or wrongly, his objective was to get us through the exam. Objectives affect both what you teach and how you teach it.

You get people through language exams by concentrating on grammar. To this day I can recite the acronyms, poems and puns that we had to memorize. DOG WUF gives you the six prepositions — Durch, Ohne, Gegen, Wider, Um, Für — that govern the accusative case in German. Give me two minutes to compose a German sentence and it will be a

"Ich werde dich immer lieben."

monument to grammatical perfection. Prepositions will govern the correct case, past participles will be sent to the end, adverbial phrases will be placed in the prescribed sequence of time, manner, place. However, conversations punctuated by two-minute gaps are hard to sustain.

On the other hand, I once taught myself basic conversational Spanish. This did not totally ignore grammar, because grammar is the set of rules which enables you to learn a lot at one go (eg. all regular -ar verbs), but getting the grammar right was subordinate to the task of going into a shop and coming out with the right food and the right change. After a month of home study, followed by a couple of weeks in Spain, I was more proficient in conversational Spanish than in German; my prospects of passing 'O' level Spanish remain minimal. Everything depends on your objective in learning the language.

If we were to write down the objectives for the above two examples we would get:

> To learn the German language sufficiently well to pass German GCSE
> To learn enough Spanish to be able to 'get by' in parts of Spain where little English is spoken.

The first of these is testable. You pass the exam, with certain grades, or you fail. It is a digital system — even if this is achieved only by setting arbitrary points on a continuum of zero to a hundred. When, or whether, the second objective is achieved is much more a matter of opinion and dependent on the standard one has set oneself. The test is not whether a sentence is grammatically correct but whether the person has made himself understood. Proficiency may be patchy. Good in shops and petrol stations but poor in a hospital. The level of success may depend as much on the listener as on the speaker.

What our language example demonstrates is that a subject that is hard from one standpoint (grammar) is soft when viewed from another — that of making oneself understood. The main difference is the level of concern about the student getting things absolutely correct. We can therefore state that how we teach a subject depends as much on the learner's objectives as on the subject matter itself. Subjects are intrinsically hard or soft, or can be broken down into hard and soft elements. What we have added is that the teaching strategy itself can be hard or soft. Figure 2.1 represents this as a matrix showing the different combinations of teaching strategy and subject matter and what they imply for the style of teaching.

Let us examine in more detail what is meant by the different combinations and see the interaction between this and the formulation of objectives. For a definition of an objective we shall use that of Mager:[1]

an intent communicated by a statement describing a proposed change

	Hard subject (subject-dependent)	Soft subject (environment/person-dependent)
Hard teaching	Rules Memorizing Complex, worked examples Hands-on/mastery	Guidelines presented as rules Samples of 'good work' 'What' more than 'how'
Soft teaching	Overview; awareness Concepts Simple examples Demonstrations	Analytical skills What questions to ask Self-awareness Discovery learning

Figure 2.1   The teaching strategy grid

in the learner. A statement of what the learner is to be like when he has successfully completed a learning experience. It is a description of a pattern of behaviour (performance) we want the learner to be able to demonstrate.

Hard/Hard

This combination of subject matter and teaching approach is that which is used when we want students to acquire specific knowledge or master a particular technique. It may partake of the nature of rote learning or drill exercises. It leads to clear, measurable objectives of the type: 'On successful conclusion of the course delegates will be able to . . .' followed by a list of the techniques they are expected to master, or facts they are expected to know, for example:

- Describe the company's major product groupings and their contribution to sales turnover.
- Construct a simple spreadsheet including text, numeric data and formulae.
- Format, edit, print and save a simple document.

Hard/Soft

This is where we are teaching a hard subject but only at the awareness level, not worrying about whether the student masters the techniques,

15

remembers all the facts or gets all the grammar correct. This leads to objectives of the sort: 'Participants will gain an understanding of . . . for example, spreadsheets as an aid to management decision-making'. The problem with objectives framed in these terms is that measuring their attainment is difficult. Half of one's audience may decide that spreadsheets are the most powerful management tool yet devised; the other half may dismiss them as a new-fangled gimmick or as beyond the intellectual capacities of their staff. *Vague objectives are an open invitation to vague teaching.* We need to harden up objectives just as we shall subsequently harden up the material. Mager is useful in this. He developed a table of vague and specific (soft and hard in our terminology) terms in formulating learning objectives:

Words open to many interpretations (soft)	Words open to fewer interpretations (hard)
to know	to write
to understand	to recite
to believe	to identify
to appreciate	to differentiate
to have faith in	to solve
to grasp the significance of	to construct
to enjoy	to list
	to compare
	to contrast

By using words from the second column rather than the first we significantly harden our objectives. Instead of 'gaining an understanding' we can say 'identify the potential and pitfalls of . . .', 'list the functions of . . .' and so on. This is much more prescriptive for the course developer. The course's specification becomes more rigorous. As a simple test of rigour we have used the extent to which different people working on the same problem achieve identical solutions. If we specify a course on spreadsheets with an objective of 'increasing understanding,' different course writers will interpret this in various ways. If our objectives are written using the terms in the right-hand list we will see a marked convergence in the courses written by different people.

Soft/Hard

Is it possible to teach soft subjects as though they were hard? The question is central to this book. I said earlier that scientific research is a process of hardening knowledge. In the so-called social sciences — roughly equivalent to interpersonal skills training in the commercial market — research is conducted in a different manner. In place of control experiments there are surveys, behavioural theories and the like. The latter can never attain the status of proof. But that is not to say that they cannot be treated as the next best thing. We should consciously strive to harden all teaching wherever possible. We should make clear at the outset the difference in status between scientific rules and behavioural 'rules'. We then teach soft subjects as hard as we can, leaving students to make the adjustments necessary in applying the 'rules' to their own environments.

How we harden up soft material is examined later in the book. Essentially it consists of developing guidelines where none existed before and in elevating existing guidelines into rules — the six principles of effective leadership. A trivial example of such a rule might be: 'Praise in public, criticize in private'. This has almost exactly the same degree of validity as: 'Never cover an honour with an honour' in bridge, 'A knight on the rim is always grim' in chess, or 'Always keep your head still' in ball games. If you follow the advice to the letter in all circumstances you will not go far wrong. But there are situations in which they may be inappropriate and experts are good enough to ignore them. You cannot say that about Pythagoras.

Hard-teaching a soft subject comes from writing objectives of the type:

Participants will learn:
● The four techniques for conducting a counselling interview . . .
● The six rules for effective telephone selling . . .

Any intellectual reservations we may entertain should be directed not at the objectives but at our level of success in hardening up the material. Is telephone selling reducible to simple rules? To what extent have we succeeded in eliminating all person-, or environment-dependent elements from career-counselling?

Soft/Soft

In teaching soft subjects hard we are attempting to translate intuition and judgement into a transmittable form. How far can we go down this particular track? One answer is given by the common expression 'painting by numbers'. The clear meaning of this is that a creative (i.e., soft) subject has been reduced to a set of rules to the point where a person of no talent is able to achieve some level of success.

The pejorative nature of the expression indicates that the process is seen as having been taken too far. Rules, even guidelines, depend for their validity upon being generally applicable. But we have previously identified environment- and person-dependent subjects which of their nature are resistant to this approach. An environment-dependent subject can be hardened up by writing a version tailored to a specific environment. This is what happens when we specify an in-company training programme and incorporate the company's own standards. A person-dependent skill can be taught one-to-one. These apart, soft subjects include too many environmental factors — and too many different types of people — for us to produce a separate hard course for every type of individual and environment. We have therefore to concede that not all subjects can be taught hard using the techniques outlined above. That is how we end up teaching people the questions to ask more than the solutions to impose. There is a corollary of this approach that not all teachers are comfortable with. If our objective is to teach people to think for themselves we must not complain if they come to conclusions different from our own!

Another problem in teaching soft topics is that we cannot arrange for students to practise what they have been taught immediately they get back to their work situation. If we are teaching word processing we can ensure that students have the opportunity to apply what they have learned before they have forgotten it. But suppose we are teaching management? One point we may cover is how to deal with a crisis. It is difficult to harden this up because crises come in many different shapes and sizes. However, we devise the guideline: In a crisis, do nothing. This is effective from the communication viewpoint because it sounds paradoxical. It is actually saying: 'Take time to analyse the situation before pressing the panic button'. Whether this is always good advice need not concern us. The point is this: we cannot arrange a crisis immediately on the student's return from the course in order to see whether he has

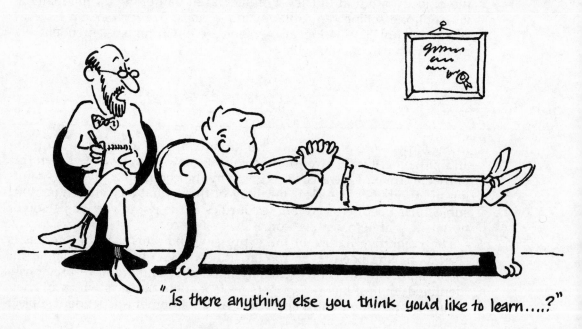

"Is there anything else you think you'd like to learn....?"

assimilated the teaching point. It may be months, or years, before a real crisis comes along. That is why a common expression on soft courses is 'planting time-bombs,' i.e., the course is educating people to cope with certain types of situations, but there is no guarantee that all or any of them may arise in the immediate future.

In teaching soft/soft we therefore have two linked problems: the absence of rules or guidelines and the unpredictability of students' opportunity to apply what they have learned. Do we therefore throw in the teaching towel and mutter 'Experience is the only teacher'? Hardly, judging by the number of management courses on offer. What then is soft/soft teaching?

A common answer is to equate it with 'discovery learning'. But this begs the question. Discovery learning is a method — it is concerned with *how* people learn. We still need to decide *what* it is that we want people to learn. If our approach is totally to let people learn for themselves without any notion of what it is we want them to learn we should be at the business end of a psychiatrist's couch, not in front of a class.

Teaching soft/soft is about people learning to think for themselves. It is also about modifying people's attitudes. The distinction between these two is enshrined in the best-known of all research about education: Bloom's taxonomy of learning.[2] This initially distinguishes between *cognitive* and *affective* learning. Cognitive learning refers to intellectual abilities such as problem-solving, remembering and reproducing knowledge. Affective means controlled by the emotions. Within the cognitive taxonomy Bloom identified a hierarchy of six steps. No higher step can be reached until one has mastered the preceding one.*

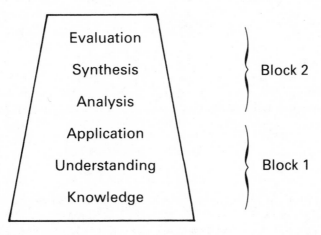

Figure 2.2   Bloom's taxonomy

*From *Taxonomy of Educational Objectives: The Classification of Educational Goals:* Handbook I. Cognitive Domain by Benjamin S. Bloom *et al.* Copyright © 1956 by Longman Inc. Reprinted by permission of Longman Inc.

19

Figure 2.2 shows these six steps divided into two blocks. Block 1 — assimilating knowledge, understanding what one has learned and being able to apply it — is predominantly hard/hard teaching. By Block 2 the skills become softer. Analysis is a problem-oriented skill — breaking down a system, problem or organization into its constituent parts. Synthesis is the ability to order individual parts into a coherent whole, thereby coming up with a solution. Evaluation is the ability to judge the rightness of a solution and to determine whether the elements fit together into a coherent and logically-sound pattern. These are the cognitive skills. If we add to the last three the affective skills of modifying people's attitudes we have identified the broad area of soft/soft teaching.

Soft/soft teaching is often an indirect process of putting people into situations loosely analogous to everyday ones and letting them draw their own conclusions. Thus people are sent on outward bound courses to learn skills of office management. This is obviously the most difficult area in which to write clear, measurable objectives. Participants will have different value systems, allied to different levels of existing skills, aptitude and experience. It is a problem one constantly comes across in soft courses. Every team leadership course has a class in which both people's starting point and personal aptitudes and attitudes vary. To take account of this we are forced to formulate the learning objective of the course as: 'To develop participants' skills in . . . motivating subordinates, decision-making and organization'. It is difficult to measure but characterizes soft/soft teaching. It is often better to allow for the difficulties of measurement by defining an overall 'aim' and then write objectives that are harder:

- To recognize the five levels of personal motivation
- To identify the four basic decision-making strategies
- To differentiate the three major organizational approaches.

In all types of training, correct objectives are of pre-eminent importance. My personal experience, as someone who has run a training company for nearly 20 years, is that failure comes as often from doing the wrong things well as from doing the right things badly.

References

1. *Preparing Instructional Objectives*, 2nd ed., Robert S. Mager, Belmont, CA, Fearon, 1975
2. *Taxonomy of Educational Objectives*, B.S. Bloom, New York, McKay, 1956

3

Who, when and where?

Once we have determined the subject matter and objectives of a course we next need to specify at whom it is directed, together with any other constraints of duration and facilities. In many instances — where, for example, the specification has arisen out of a formal training needs analysis — the people at whom the course is aimed are already broadly identified.

The audience

Students' appraisals frequently exhibit a wide spread of opinion between people on the same course. They have listened to the same lectures, done the same exercises, worked through the same case studies; yet their opinions of the course can range from 'excellent' to 'poor'. What accounts for such divergent opinions? Is it not possible to please all the people all the time?

The key point is the *divergence* of opinion. If a course is badly designed, written or presented, evaluations will show a degree of unanimity. But when there are divergent opinions it usually comes down to one of two things. Either the style of the course or lecturer has prompted different responses, or different students were looking for different things from the course. The first of these is a design or presentation problem which will be examined later in the book. The second is a specification problem. The course appraisal form should be designed so as to distinguish between these. What concentrates attention on the specification is responses of the type: 'The course was not very useful to me personally . . .' These can easily coexist with favourable comments about the lecturer himself. Good marks for the instructor, combined with low marks for the relevance of the course or, to a lesser extent, adverse comments about the pace, are an indication that a student is on the wrong course. It is the function of the specification to ensure that this does not happen by closely identifying the target audience. Just as with the subject matter of the course, the specification of the audience must exclude as well as include. It is as important to specify who should not attend the course, as who should. Many instructors would argue that it is more important!

What characteristics of the audience do we include in our specification? We need first to draw a distinction between an audience — a collection of individuals — and the individuals that comprise the audience. This is important because some characteristics apply at the group level and others at the individual level. The only true group characteristics are:

- The size of the audience
- The homogeneity of the audience

The most important individual characteristics are people's prior knowledge, aptitude and attitude. We can classify these as group attributes only by introducing qualifiers such as the 'general' level of knowledge or the 'average' level of experience. The latter are typically the attributes among which we are seeking homogeneity. We seldom need to specify the sex, religion, height, physical condition or age of participants unless the character of the training (e.g. outward bound-style courses) makes them relevant.

Size

The size of the audience is vital in any training situation and must, therefore, be part of the specification. The bigger the audience is, the more any communication is going to be one-way; the smaller, the more opportunity of personal tuition. Almost always the pressure is to put more people on a course than is optimum from the teaching standpoint. This is simply because, for an in-company course it reduces the per capita training cost. For a commercial training company running public courses, the profitability of a given course is a function of the number of people who attend. In this situation there is a great temptation, particularly rife in the marketing department, to cast the net as wide as possible. This can be seen in leaflets containing a clear and specific description of whom the course is intended for: 'This course is aimed at internal auditors, accountants, investment analysts,' but which then goes on: '*and any other persons with an interest in the application of computers to financial matters*'. The italicized phrase is equivalent to saying 'and anyone else who'll pay'. It may maximize course numbers — and thereby, short-term profit for a commercial training company — but its wide net risks gathering in people for whom the relevance of the course is marginal. The moral for commercial training companies is to keep a firm hand on the marketing people.

The bigger the audience is, the more any
communication is going to be one-way

Homogeneity

The prior level of knowledge of students is much less important than that it should be uniform across the class. English can be taught in remedial classes or at degree level. What cannot be done is to teach both together. It is therefore necessary to specify what prerequisites are necessary for attendance on the course (and, as always, what are not — 'no prior knowledge of computers is required'). This is often done by describing certain levels of attainment or by specifying job titles or grades — with the caveat that the latter can frequently conceal wide differences between or within different companies.

It is impossible to specify students' level of motivation in coming on the course so that the instructor is always likely to be faced with differing attitudes. If only a specification could say: 'People attending this course should have a genuine interest in the subject allied to a real willingness to learn'!

23

Time

No matter how talented and motivated you may be, it takes time to learn to play a musical instrument. A crash two-day course will not leave you able to play Mendelssohn's violin concerto. If you think this is another statement of the obvious, consider how many short commercial courses attempt to teach similar skills. Two-day courses on effective writing abound. Yet, unless you regard writing as an activity reducible to a few simple rules, you cannot make any significant impact on a person's ability to write in less than six months. The six months does not mean a continuous course. In common with piano-playing, skiing or typing, writing demands a high ratio of practice to tuition. The six months can be 26 one-hour lessons interspersed with much practical work.

Examination of the subject matter and learning objectives can lead to a formulation of the ideal timing. This, as we have seen, is a combination of the total time required and the time-scheduling. Both are often constrained. Much instructor-based training has to be continuous. Most commercial training consists of getting together a group of people for a course of one or more days. There are almost certainly costs involved in getting people to the course venue and in dislocation of working. This militates against education as an on-going activity in favour of 'one-shot' learning.

Where training is continuous, the commonest problem is lack of time. The important thing about specifying a course is to bring all such problems into the open and then sort out which are negotiable. If time is non-negotiable (senior managers cannot be spared for more than two days) we must cut our suit according to our cloth. This normally means leaving things out or softening the approach. The only other alternative is to stretch the cloth a bit by negotiating a lengthening of the course day.

We can represent insufficient time by drawing boxes to represent time needed and time available for a course on communication skills, as seen in Figure 3.1. The most satisfactory solution is to negotiate additional time, in other words making the 'available' box equal in size to the 'required' box. If this cannot be done, something has to give. Diagrammatically, we can take either a horizontal slice off the 'time required' box by eliminating one complete topic (see third box), or we can retain all the topics but reduce the depth to which they are taught (see fourth box). This is represented diagrammatically by taking a vertical slice off the 'time required' box.

The extent of the mismatch between time available and time required will only be established during the next phase. However, an experienced designer should have a good 'feel' for this even at the specification phase or as soon as possible into the design process. In practice, the solution is often a combination of all three — some more time is made available, a topic discarded, others pruned back. What is important is that these

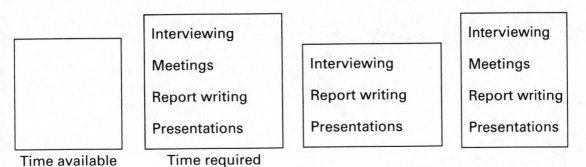

Figure 3.1 **Matching course contents to time**

compromises should be made at the specification phase. Continuing with detailed design and writing without sorting this out merely results in an arbitrary cutting back at the presentation phase. Put more simply, the lecturer runs out of time. Instead of a considered view about which topics should be cut back, the last topic on the timetable will be rushed through at breakneck speed.

Facilities

A lesson that I have learned painfully over the years is that if students on the first day of a course have reason to complain about the facilities — lack of space, noise, lukewarm coffee — by the second day they will be thinking the course is not that hot either. It is difficult to overemphasize the importance of good training facilities. The best instructor struggles when faced with a noisy, overheated and crowded room, or with equipment that continually goes wrong.

The specification must therefore identify the type of facilities and equipment required for successful running of the course, detailing whether the course is to be held on-site or off-site; residential or non-residential. Is the training room a proper lecture room or a general meeting room being pressed into service? The size and facilities of the lecture room are of the utmost importance. It needs to be large enough to allow ample space for the audience, quiet and the right temperature. Too many times we lecture in a room where air-conditioning consists in opening the windows, whereupon one is drowned by the noise from outside.

In writing the specification we are forced to make some judgement about how the course will be run in order to identify the facilities required. If it is going to be run workshop style there is likely to be a requirement for additional 'break-out' rooms. If so, how many are needed and is this number available? Will the presenter have access to training aids such as a video-recorder, an overhead projector, or a television? Will the students need special equipment? It is not difficult to lay hands on one of each of the necessary items for the course; it may be much more difficult where one for each student is required.

Course structure

Sometimes a specification will give the designer complete freedom to develop the course. On other occasions there may be existing course material which needs to be included. In the extreme situation a lecturer may be asked to present a specific course, working from material written by other people: 'Head Office is implementing this new set of standards worldwide — here is the training programme that goes along with it'. If strictly adhered to, such an instruction completely bypasses the specification, design and writing processes. However, in practice, it would be most unusual — as well as unwise — for this to happen. It presupposes that the material can be taught identically anywhere in the world, to any type of audience. If the type of material is such that the role of the instructor is reduced to mouthing words and putting up visuals written by someone else, without any contribution of his own, head office would have done better to have produced a film or some form of self-instruction programme. If, on the other hand, there are environment- or person-dependent aspects to the course, then a specification must be written and the existing material examined in the light of this specification. Such material may well be incorporated in large measure — on the principle of not re-inventing the wheel — but the trainer will retain the freedom to redesign and rewrite to fit the course to the local needs.

In any field, a specification can be looked upon as a statement of what the user wants within constraints regarding how the 'wants' are satisfied. Definition of the subject area, audience and objectives define what is wanted; identification of available time, facilities and equipment tend to define limits on how the course designer meets the specification. They are constraints on his freedom. Frequently the constraints imposed on a training programme make full achievement of the objectives impossible. In this case either the specification is re-negotiated — more time, smaller audience, better facilities — or the objectives are modified. But any such compromise must be made early in the development process. For this reason it is vital that constraints are exposed, clarified and negotiated as part of the specification process.

4

Teaching circles

Let us now pull together the various elements of course specification. The hard/soft analysis is invaluable to the course specifier and subsequently to the designer. Despite my best endeavours it is a soft technique (mainly because specifying courses is environment-specific). It therefore tells you what questions you need to ask rather than providing a set of answers. Nevertheless, a significant theme of this book is the need to harden up wherever we can — always with the caveat that in so doing we may dilute the intellectual purity of the message. So we should try to do this with the specification phase.

As we have seen, a common method of hardening up is to represent as black and white what is in fact a continuum. We can employ this ourselves to invent a convenient notation with which to embody the ideas of the preceding chapters. To do this I shall revert to the analysis into subject-, environment- and person-dependent topics but represent them as discrete sets. The validity of this analysis is shown by the ease with which they map on to the different teaching approaches of training, educating and coaching.

1. *Training* is the teaching of facts, clear rules or defined techniques or skills. It is subject-dependent and fits squarely into our hard/hard combination.
2. *Education* means literally 'leading people out'. It is concerned with enhancing people's ability to think for themselves. It relates predominantly to environment-dependent material.
3. *Coaching* is person-dependent. It assumes that the student has some pre-existing skill or experience in the particular area and aims to *develop* it from that starting point. Indeed, were this book aimed exclusively at the business training market, I would use the term 'development'. The notion of taking existing skills and enhancing these explains why golf pros and tennis coaches always ask you to 'hit a few balls first'.

Using a pie chart (see Figure 4.1), we can represent pictorially the relative proportions of the three approaches on a course, or part of a

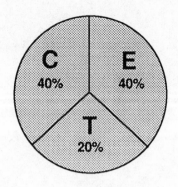

Figure 4.1 Teaching circle

course. It is useful initially as a specification aid. Subsequently it acts as a descriptor for potential students by showing the type of teaching approach they will meet on the course. Let us examine some examples.

Example 1: report writing
Imagine that a commercial training company is specifying a two-day course on report writing. It is to be specified as a public course, although it will be available to be run in-company. The fact that it is specified as a public course means that people from different backgrounds will be taught. Their companies may be small or large, in the public or private sector, service industry or product-based. They may, or may not, have their own standards for formatting and writing reports. The reports could be sales-oriented, technical or instructive.

Since all these considerations influence the way in which reports are written, the course cannot be dogmatic on the question of standards, layouts and writing styles. For an in-company course it is possible to be more specific and the teaching circle would be different (having a higher 'T' content). As it is, the course will have a high 'E' content reflecting the environment-dependent nature of much of what is being taught.

However, it is accepted that people like to be taught hard. The course should therefore include as many rules, guidelines, tips and checklists as possible. By specifying a substantial 'T' content, the course designer is forced to locate or develop these. The type of content which would result would be techniques such as the fog index, rules for spelling, abbreviations, correct usage, recommended layouts for different types of reports, how to compile an index and so on.

The third element in our teaching circle is coaching or personal development. Participants on the course will have different writing abilities and different levels of experience. If someone's writing ability is really to be improved, it will be necessary to work with him individually. Handing out examples of good and bad writing is a poor substitute. However, the amount of personal attention that can be given on any course is a function of the number of people attending and the time

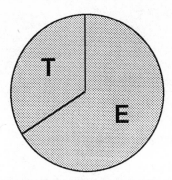

Figure 4.2 Teaching circle — report writing

available. In this example we assume that we have only two days and up to 16 people will be accepted. In so doing, the possibility of individualized attention has been precluded. If the designer thinks that this is no way to run a writing course he must do what all designers in similar situations do — renegotiate the specification. As it is, the teaching circle, by containing no C element, warns people not to expect this type of teaching. (See Figure 4.2.)

Example 2: project management
Course specification is not always a blank-canvas exercise. Sometimes we need to respecify a course as a result of changing circumstances. This happened once to my own company. In response to a request from a client to develop a project management course for them, we substantially rewrote an existing public course. In so doing we put in new techniques for estimating, collection of project metrics and project tracking using a software package. The resulting course was well received not only by the original client but also by other companies operating in the same field.

What more obvious than to incorporate the new material into the public version of the course? The problem that arose was that the public course started to receive lower markings from students, mainly on the issue of how useful the course had been to them — a sure sign of a problem with the specification. The variable was the audience. Companies taking the course in-house had committed themselves to a decision to implement the techniques taught; students on the public course had no such commitment.

Hence the techniques were of little relevance. What they were looking for were skills such as how to renegotiate a deadline, how to influence both their bosses and their subordinates. It could legitimately be argued that the difference between the two courses would show up in the different syllabuses. There is obviously some truth in this, but a revised teaching circle is much clearer. The new course had a teaching circle which was predominantly 'T'. The public course was later rewritten to

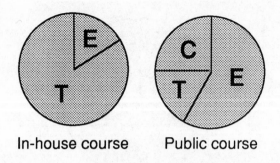

In-house course   Public course

Figure 4.3   Teaching circles — project management

emphasize the 'E' and 'C' aspects, particularly of interpersonal skills. (See Figure 4.3.)

If we are specifying a course that embraces a diversity of topics, different teaching circles may be needed for each one. Thus a course on improving communication skills, embracing interviewing, meetings, training, writing and presentations, could well have a number of teaching circles reflecting the different approaches to be employed to the different topics. The teaching circle thus exerts an influence on design, writing and presentation. This will be explored in detail throughout the book but the importance of teaching circles can be gauged by a preliminary analysis of what they tell us about a course.

Instructor skills

The teaching circle gives an accurate guide to the type of skills and experience required of the course instructor. High 'T' courses are highly-structured. Their design and writing is of great significance. If these are done well the course can be run by instructors with a relatively narrow range of expertise and experience. What matters is that the instructor can rescue the student from a 'fatal error' message on his screen, not his ability to indulge in a philosophical discussion of the respective merits of different programming languages.

On the other hand, courses with high 'E' content require breadth, more than depth, of knowledge and experience. This reflects the likelihood of students asking questions of the sort 'How does what you're saying relate to . . .?' 'A problem we've had is . . . how do we solve that?'. A high 'C' rating indicates the need for an instructor skilled at sizing up and analysing people's strengths and weaknesses. He must be sympathetic, diplomatic and able to think on his feet. Thus, whereas a well-written 'T' course is already most of the way towards ensuring success, 'E' and 'C' courses still depend to a significant extent on the skills of the presenter.

Class size

High 'E' courses need to be interactive; otherwise the student is as well off reading a book on the subject. Class size is therefore limited by the amount of interaction that one anticipates. At a conference this may be restricted to a couple of questions from the audience at the end — which is why I regard most conferences more as social/marketing than teaching events. In this situation you can have as large an audience as you wish. It works as long as questions asked are of equal relevance to all members of the audience; as soon as anyone puts a question that is specific to their own environment the rest of the audience switches off. When running 'E' courses I prefer not to have more than 16 participants in order to give everyone the opportunity to participate. High 'T' courses will usually be smaller, reflecting the requirement for practical work to make sure that the student masters the techniques. There may also be tests to administer to make sure that knowledge has been acquired. Technology, such as different forms of teaching machines, may make larger classes possible. 'Coaching' by my definition is a one-to-one activity (though others may learn from the victim's success or failure) and therefore demands small classes.

Most courses contain a mixture of the different approaches. This impacts on course design. A lecturer can impart the principles of interviewing to a class of 20; if he then wants to give practice, through role-playing, he will need to call in additional people to assist or set the students to interview each other.

Course sequence

With 'E' courses the standard sequence is for the instructor to introduce a topic with an explanation and then initiate a discussion. The interesting contrast is between 'T' and 'C' approaches. Training consists of explaining a technique or skill and then giving exercises, case studies and tests to make sure that it has been grasped. With coaching, as we shall see, 'doing' typically precedes teaching.

In-company vs. public courses

As remarked earlier, in-company courses should have a higher 'T' content than the equivalent public course. This is because we are reducing to one the number of environments at which the teaching is directed. Material can be tailored to company standards thereby eliminating the consideration of alternatives (with the consequent obligation on the student to choose between them when applying the technique). Also, within an in-company setting one can be reasonably confident that techniques taught will be applied and standards implemented.

Duration of effect

Facts and skills are forgotten quickly if not used. Techniques such as book-keeping, designing data bases or using a sextant are likely to decay. It is thus essential that any 'T' course teaches only skills that will be put to immediate use. Again, this may appear to be a statement of the obvious but I never cease to be surprised by the number of students attending my company's courses who have no immediate plans to use the knowledge thus acquired.

The exception to this rule are neuro-muscular skills such as riding a bicycle. These may become 'rusty' but they are seldom lost once acquired. One can explain this by classing these as skills which are developed through coaching more than training.

Education is of its nature much longer-lasting. Five years after finishing my philosophy course at university I discovered how applicable the study of philosophy was to systems analysis. This is because the common denominator is the need to think clearly. If we can teach people to think analytically, or to think creatively, we have imparted a skill that will be useful throughout their life.

Quality assurance

The hard/soft analysis will often reveal the source of problems in courses. If the evaluation form includes questions about the usefulness of the course, a low mark indicates a wrong specification. Relevance can often be enhanced by increasing the 'T' or 'C' content at the expense of 'E'. One learns to become suspicious of courses with a very high 'E' content. The danger is that such courses put too much emphasis on problems and too little on solutions. People go away from them with a warm feeling that everyone is in the same boat but without specific guidance as to what to do about it. It is better to be categoric — at the risk of being proved wrong in some circumstances — than to deal in such a high level of generalities that no one can possibly dispute them. The higher the level, the more is left to the person to decide when applying the techniques or guidelines. It is the function of course writing to reduce this gap by hardening up the material.

In determining the teaching circle we complete the course specification. The user has specified what he wants taught and to whom, and has given an indication of the type of approach that he wishes to see. But he has not pre-empted the design decisions. This is an important principle. Course design is a specialized activity calling for creativity and for a broad knowledge and understanding of the many different teaching methods and aids. The person specifying the course should know what he wants; it is for the designer to decide how best this can be achieved.

An effective means of producing consistency when we are teaching questions rather than answers is to devise forms for people to complete. Showing completed versions of such forms has the added benefit of providing a working example of the approach. As will be seen in Chapter 8, explanation by example is a basic teaching technique. Figure 4.4 shows a completed specification form for a 'Training the Trainers' course. We shall follow the development of this course throughout the remainder of the book.

SPECIFICATION FORM

Course title   Training the Trainers

Aims of course

The course aims to teach participants a structured approach to course development and presentation.

Relationship to other courses

The course uses material on presentation techniques which is also used in 'Improving Communication Skills'.

Objectives

On successful completion of the course the student will be able to:

describe the four phases of specification, design, writing and presentation;

write a clear specification for course development;

construct a course design and break this into individual sessions;

write teaching material, including students' notes, visuals and exercises.

This course is intended to enhance students' abilities to:

develop interesting and effective courseware by use of varying types of material and teaching approach;

run effective learning programmes in a variety of teaching modes

Target audience

Aimed at: Experienced and novice trainers, full-time and part-time whether involved in technical or behavioural training.

Minimum/maximum size   Nine students with one presenter; 16 with two

Specified prerequisites   None

Prior knowledge/experience or job groupings

Demonstrated ability to communicate both verbally and in writing

Constraints

Scheduled first run of course   September 19XX

Development budget   36 days

Course time available:

Number of days   4   Number of hours per day   8

Is the course continuous/non-continuous?   continuous

Figure 4.4   Completed Specification form

Availability of:
Students   Subject to existing lecturing commitments at the
             time
Trainers   As scheduled
Are trainers—experts in the subject matter of course/experienced
in teaching techniques?
   Yes

Existing courseware/background material:
   Presentation and creative writing sessions from 'Improving
   Communications Skills'.
   Refer attached book list.

Facilities required (delete/specify as applicable)
Residential/non residential/self study   Residential
Own training facilities/external   External; lecture room plus two
                                   break-out rooms

Equipment required
Overhead projectors/flip chart—paper—crayons/35 mm projector/
video-recorder/TV Video camera/micro computers/~~Interactive~~
~~video~~
Other (please specify)   One computer per syndicate; two OHPs/
                         cameras if more than nine students

Other requirements:
Will the course be run in different locations (specify)   London
                                                          only
Should it include social activities (specify)   No organized activities

Syllabus (topics covered)
   Preparation: knowing your material—hard/soft analysis
   Objectives: setting clear objectives, relationship to audience
   and material
   Audience: defining the target audience
   Teaching circles: education, training and coaching, relevance
   to course specification and design
   Course design: breaking into sessions, session objectives,
   sequencing
   Session planning: passive/participative, permanent/non-
   permanent courseware, use of training aids
   Course writing: handouts, visuals, exercises, case studies
   Presentation: teaching styles, motivation, encouraging par-
   ticipation, handling questions, typical presentation problems

Teaching circle
Training 30   Education 45   Coaching 25

Figure 4.4   Completed Specification form _concluded_

Part II
Designing the course

Central to the approach advocated in this book is the concept of breaking course development into defined phases. To perform each phase requires some knowledge of its succeeding phase. Without this we specify something incapable of design, or design what cannot be written. This is typically achieved either by one person being knowledgeable about both phases or by consultation. Each phase then validates the contents of the preceding phase before going on to implement them. Provided this is properly done, the developer should not have to backtrack more than one phase. In other words, it is perfectly legitimate for the specification to be modified during design, and for the design to be modified during writing but one should not have to change the specification as a result of session writing or the design as a result of presenting. Costs are incurred whenever we are forced to backtrack more than one phase as it inevitably results in destroying work already done to a detailed level. Because course development is still primarily an art, this is bound to happen occasionally, but the aim of following a formalized method is to make this the exception rather than the rule.

Partitioning course development confers a number of other significant benefits:

- It encourages and facilitates involvement of the user of the training throughout the course development by presenting him with clear deliverables from each phase.
- Quality assurance can be applied to the outputs of course design and writing. This replaces the common system whereby once the specification has been agreed the user forgets all about it until the first course and then complains that the end-product is not what he had in mind!
- Misunderstandings between different people involved in the development are brought out and resolved before effort is expended on work which has subsequently to be discarded.
- It enables the course designer to make the big decisions and then delegate session writing to other people whilst remaining in overall control of the development.
- It explicitly recognizes an important but often overlooked point — that different people are better at some phases than at others. Frequently we tend to assume that the best presenter is automatically the best course designer and writer. This is often far from the truth.

The design phase is broken into two processes — macro-design and session planning. Macro-design consists of translating the specification into a coherent sequence of timed sessions, each of which has its own mini-specification itemizing what is to be covered, the teaching objectives and teaching approach.

Session planning takes each session and produces a detailed writing plan for:

- Handouts
- Practical work
- Visuals
- Presenter's guide.

However, before making a start on design, we need to be aware of how people like to learn.

5
Writing for your audience

The cardinal rule of communication is: 'Write for your audience'. In designing a course we therefore need to think not only about the characteristics of the subject matter but also about our audience. In Chapter 3 I said that it is meaningless to talk of an audience's attitude. You can only talk of the attitudes or preferences of the individual members of the audience and hope that they are reasonably homogeneous. The specification lays down the target size and prior knowledge of the audience, but it cannot specify personalities — 'This course is to be written for extroverts'. Yet people's personalities and the style of learning they prefer are of vital importance in the success of a course. Since people's preferences are different we should aim to construct a course that has 'something in it' for everyone.

By 'preference' I mean the teaching approach that a student is most comfortable with and finds most productive. I can best illustrate this by a true story. I was running a course on training needs analysis for a multinational computer company. The audience consisted of customer training managers from most western European countries. As I explained the system of training needs analysis that they would be expected to use, one of the participants demurred on the ground that the system was too inflexible. His customers, he said with an expressive shrug of the shoulders, expected to be treated as individuals. Another participant took immediate issue with this and complained that, on the contrary, the system was far too flexible. He had come on the course hoping to receive a package of standard documents that he could immediately use. Was it a coincidence that the first person was from Spain and the second from Germany? To avoid accusations of racism I shall employ an even more sweeping generalization: the farther north and east you travel in the world, the more people like to be taught hard; the farther south and west, the greater the preference for soft. My experience is that Germans and Scandinavians are more precise than, say, Latin races and, as a direct result, favour hard teaching; Arabs and Chinese have a cultural and educational background of learning by rote and prefer hard teaching for that reason.

Whilst in generalization mode I would make a further claim. The more experienced a person is in the subject matter of the course, the more he prefers to be taught soft. He has his own views and likes the idea of being invited to think for himself and come to his own conclusions. However, as soon as we revert to a subject matter with which he has little familiarity, he wants to be taught hard. If I personally went on a course on creative writing I would feel patronized if the teacher gave me the six golden rules of writing. But on a one-day seminar on direct marketing I avidly lapped up tips such as: 'Always put a postscript on a direct mail letter', 'Always include a covering letter with any leaflet'.

The above two generalizations affect the way in which we design and write courses. Suppose that you reject them (I constantly acknowledge that course development is soft). If you do, I suspect it is not because you wish to substitute even more sweeping generalizations of your own ('All left-handed people prefer soft teaching'), but because your view is that we should think of people as individuals. Good. In that case, we need to be aware of individuals' preferred learning styles in order that we can accommodate them.

Starting with Hippocrates in 400 BC, there have been many attempts to identify and classify people's styles and temperaments. Hippocrates designated people's personalities as: sanguine, melancholic, choleric, phlegmatic. In the 1920s Carl Jung developed 'psychological types' to describe how people interact with each other. He called these types: feelers, thinkers, sensors, intuitive.

Latterly, similar attempts have been made to identify people's preferred learning styles. Kolb[1] identified four main types of learner — converger, diverger, assimilator, accommodator — and used a learning style inventory to establish an individual's relative emphasis on each of the four styles. Peter Honey and Alan Mumford,[2] two British management trainers, identify activists, reflectors, theorists and pragmatists. They use a questionnaire which tests your agreement or disagreement with statements such as:

- I actively seek out new experiences
- I am careful not to jump to conclusions too quickly
- I like to relate my actions to a general principle
- In discussions I like to get straight to the point
- I like to run meetings on methodical lines
- Most times I believe the end justifies the means
- I enjoy being the one that talks a lot
- I often get irritated by people who want to rush headlong into things.

Based on responses to these, a person's learning style quotient (LSQ) is derived which is their scores in each of the four categories. The book then relates the LSQ to the type of learning that appeals most to each type:

1. *Activists* learn best from activities (amongst others) where:

   ● There are new experiences/problems/opportunities from which to learn
   ● They can engross themselves in games, competitive teamwork tasks, role-playing exercises
   ● They are thrown in at the deep end, and set a challenge.

They react against:

● Passive learning
● Solitary work such as reading, writing, thinking on their own
● Attention to detail.

2. *Reflectors* learn best when:

   ● They are allowed to think over activities
   ● They can carry out detailed research
   ● They have an opportunity to review what has happened, what they have learned.

They react against:

● Being forced into the limelight

Typical activist learning style.

- Being given insufficient data on which to base a conclusion
- Having to take short cuts or carry out a superficial job.

3. *Theorists* learn best from activities where:

   - What is being taught is part of a system, model, concept or theory
   - They are in structured situations with a clear purpose
   - They are offered interesting ideas and concepts even though they are not immediately relevant.

They react against:

- Being pitchforked into doing something without a context or apparent purpose
- Being unsure whether the subject matter is methodologically sound
- Having to participate in a situation emphasizing emotions and feelings.

4. *Pragmatists* learn best from activities where:

   - There is an obvious link between the subject matter and a problem or opportunity on the job
   - They are given immediate opportunities to implement what they have learned
   - They have the chance to try out and practise techniques with coaching/feedback from a credible expert.

They react against:

- Learning that seems distant from reality, i.e., 'ivory towered', all theory and general principles
- The feeling that people are going round in circles without getting anywhere fast enough
- Being offered no apparent reward for the learning activity, i.e., more sales, shorter meetings, higher bonuses, promotion.

Honey and Mumford's book includes an interesting analysis of the scores of different occupational groups. Salesmen score (out of a maximum of 20 for each category) — activist: 13.3, reflector: 11.5, theorist: 11.4, pragmatist: 14.1. It follows that if we are designing a sales course we should provide challenging exercises closely related to their work environment. Accountants, on the other hand score — activist: 7.0, reflector: 14.9, theorist: 14.5, pragmatist: 15.3 — generally preferring a course that explains basic principles and allows them to think through in detail what has been taught. Trainers score — activist: 11.2, reflector:

12.9, theorist: 11.4, pragmatist: 12.4. Although trainers' activist score is the lowest of the four, it is the second highest of all the occupational groups surveyed, exceeded only by salesmen.

At a more general level, what it provides the course designer with is empirical evidence of the wide spectrum of different approaches that people have to learning. We all have a natural tendency to assume that everyone will enjoy, and respond to, the type of learning that we prefer ourselves. There is thus a danger that we design courses in our own image. I scored high on 'activist'. The 'credit' side of the activists' training approach is:

- Giving a positive and encouraging lead in short-term learning activities
- Responding spontaneously to opportunities as they arise.

Against this, however, must be set the fact that activists are less likely to:

- Provide planned learning experiences
- Give support to learning as a planned learning activity
- Give different learning experiences to people with different learning styles.

My own courses have always tended to reflect my enthusiasm for throwing people in at the deep end. As a result of being made aware of different learning styles I now try to vary the type of learning experience with particular reference to the preferences of reflectors and theorists. The descriptors of the different preferences of the four styles act as a checklist against which to review a course. This is most easily done at the design and writing stages when you have the time to review what you have written in order to balance the educational approaches. However, a knowledge of learning styles is of obvious use to the presenter as he can still choose to emphasize or play down certain aspects of the material.

The course designer is the key element in creatively welding together the many options into a cohesive and enjoyable course which meets the specification. He will do this by:

- Combining hard and soft material in proportions dictated by the nature of the subject and the target audience.
- Writing passive and participative sessions in proportions dictated by the amount of course time available and the learning objectives and teaching circle.

In this he should take notice of the following guidelines:

- For every person who complains that a subject was taught too hard, ten will complain that it was not hard enough.

- For every person who complains that the course was too participative, ten will complain that it was not participative enough.

References

1. *Learning Cycle and Learning Style Inventory*, D.A. Kolb, Experiential Learning, Prentice-Hall, 1984
2. *Manual of Learning Styles*: Honey, Peter and Mumford, Alan. Peter Honey, Maidenhead, 1986. (Purchasing the book carries the entitlement to reproduce the tests)

6

Macro-design

'Design' is an interesting word. The adjective with which you qualify it serves largely to define the extent to which it is seen as an art or a science, soft or hard. Most people would, without formal instruction, consider themselves competent to undertake interior design, at least for themselves. Some would go further and consider their own efforts superior to those of professional interior designers. Few people, on the other hand, would offer to design a nuclear power station.

Where on this typical hard/soft continuum is course design? I would designate it as soft of centre on the grounds that course developers can make a reasonable stab at it without the benefit of prior instruction. What a formal method should do is to 'harden up' course design, thereby making success less person-dependent.

There is a variety of ways in which we can achieve this. The first is to impose a semi-formal structure by defining a set of processes through which the designer must go. These are:

1. Examine the course topics in detail, deciding how they will be taught and allocating time against them.
2. Break the course into sessions. For each session specify:
   - Objectives
   - Material to be covered
   - Teaching methods
   - Time available.
3. Sequence the sessions.
4. Link the sessions together and construct the course timetable.

Sometimes two of the above processes may be combined, particularly for a relatively small amount of course development or where the designer and writer is the same person.

Examine the course topics

The specification defines the content of the course as a list of topics and sub-topics. Thus a specification on interviewing skills might contain:

- Different interview situations
- The importance of preparation
- Writing an interview guide
- Conducting the interview
- Questioning techniques
- Dealing with the awkward interviewee.
- Note-taking
- Interview summaries

This is a perfectly acceptable level of detail for a specification. In turning it into a design, the designer will want to explore what the user means by 'different interview situations'. Are counselling, recruitment and investigative interviews all included and are they all to be given equal weight? Should there be practical work — if so, in class, in groups or at an individual level? Where do individual topics fit within the hard/soft classification? Such questions force a detailed dialogue between the person commissioning the course and the person designing it. It is vital that a clear understanding is arrived at between them before any design is undertaken.

Break the course into sessions

The above analysis allows the designer to determine the amount of time needed to cover the topic to the depth required. Having done this for all listed topics the designer can arrive at a total estimated time for the course. It is at this point that the compromises mentioned in Chapter 3 are most likely to be made if the total estimated time exceeds the time available. The designer should also check for 'overload' — that the course is not trying to teach too many new things at the same time. Before breaking the course into sessions he may want to split it into two separate courses. This is often particularly relevant to courses teaching neuro-muscular skills where the student needs to consolidate on basic skills before moving on to more advanced ones.

If the estimated time for a session is greater than an hour and a half the designer should consider splitting the session into two. ('Consider' is a deplorably soft word to use. A method is much more impressive-sounding for being more categoric. But design is still soft and there may be cogent reasons for not splitting a session.) Finally, timed sessions are converted to a course timetable.

In many cases the designer, writer and presenter are all the same person. This makes communication much simpler but often leads to course documentation being neglected. It is kept in the one person's head. The only documentation available subsequently is the end-product — students' manual and course exercises. No presenter's guide is written. There is no 'audit trail' showing how the course was developed. In the absence of this it becomes much more difficult to maintain and enhance the course. For this reason it is a good discipline to separate the phases of development, and document them as you go. Standardization of the activity can be enforced by means of a design form as illustrated by Figure 6.3 at the end of this chapter.

Sequence the sessions

Correct sequence is the basis of all effective communication. To prove this one need only study the media. If you read a newspaper account of a sporting event you find that more often than not it does not follow the strict sequence in which the events occurred. It starts not at the beginning of the day's play but at the most critical point in the proceedings — the vital goal, the dubious line-call, the decisive innings. The sequence of the story is not the same as the sequence of the events being reported. Why is this? It is because the reporter has to compete for our attention. This is even more true of television and radio where people quickly turn to another channel if they find the first few seconds uninteresting. Because the reporter needs to engage our attention he puts the most interesting part at the start of the article. Stylistically, this leaves him a problem since if he now continues chronologically, he will end up at the point where he began. Ending articles, television sketches and lectures is seldom easy.

The reason people feel confident to design courses without formal training is that the question of the sequence of sessions can be treated intuitively or by opting for what seems to be the obvious solution. To harden this up we need to identify as many different alternatives as possible with guidelines as to when each is appropriate. In so doing we may merely be putting names on things that experienced trainers already do intuitively, but codification and dissemination of intuitively-developed good practices is one of the most important aspects of any teaching. In seeking to tabulate different sequences I have identified the following common approaches. Those in the first list can be used at the level of both course design and session planning.

- Random
- Chronological
- Dependent
- Top-down
- Teach, then do
- Do, then teach.

The following are more generally applicable at the session planning level only:

- Problem to solution
- Familiar to unfamiliar
- Explain the purpose
- First things first.

Random

The simplest place from which to start is the assumption of no particular sequence. Some courses consist of a set of independent topics for which there is no strikingly obvious reason to put one topic before any other. When teaching biology it may matter little in which order we teach respiration, circulation and the central nervous system. But it turns out to be very difficult to find a subject where no sequence is preferable to any other. The nearest I have come to this in commercial training is an orientation course for expatriates going to work abroad for the first time. The information they need is reasonably discrete: climate, currency, religion, history, business laws, and so on. There is no immediately self-evident reason for timetabling any one topic before any other. However, groups to whom I have set this exercise invariably find some reason for putting one topic ahead of another. The litmus test is whether, during course design, the designer is willing to put topics on pieces of paper and draw them out of a hat. Not many pass this test. We may regard a random sequence as what computer people call the 'default option', i.e., what you get if no other sequence is specified.

Chronological

Let us turn from biology to history. Below is a list of five historical events:

- Russian Revolution
- Versailles Peace Treaty
- Wall Street Crash
- Spanish Civil War
- Invasion of Czechoslovakia.

A school's modern history syllabus includes the above five topics. A student has missed half a term through illness. As he returns, the class has reached the Wall Street Crash. He has no particular problems in doing his homework because the Wall Street Crash can be understood independently of the Russian Revolution or the Versailles Peace Treaty.

Much teaching sensibly follows the sequence in which things happen in real life. This book follows the sequence whereby courses are specified, designed, written and presented. However, I could equally well explain this sequence by pointing out that the later topics only become meaningful as a result of the earlier. It is futile to teach someone to design a system, or a training programme, if they have not first grasped the importance of getting the specification right. The later activities *depend* on the earlier.

Dependent

Back to school. Our student, having successfully resumed his history studies, moves on to his next lesson — mathematics. Now he has problems. Whereas one can write sensibly about the Spanish Civil War without knowing anything about the Wall Street Crash, it is difficult to do quadratic equations if you cannot solve $2y + 10 = 20$.

Most complex subjects are like this. Where there is a dependency of this nature, the instructor has to ensure that his audience has grasped steps 1 to 3 before going on to step 4. Feedback is essential. Without it we think we are explaining things beautifully until someone asks a question which shows that he got lost four hours before.

One of the problems of dependency sequencing is that a class will tend to advance at the pace of the slowest. In schools this is avoided by streaming according to ability. On commercial courses this option is not possible. We should think about writing material in such a way as to reduce the dependency effect. This can be done by building in check-points at which everyone can be given handouts — of partial solutions — that bring them back into synchronization.

An alternative that, unfortunately, one often sees is to press on regardless — to complete the syllabus even though vital topics are not being grasped. Bridge classes are often like this. There is no point in soldiering on through a syllabus, finally arriving at slam-bidding, if people have failed to grasp the basics of playing the hand. Nevertheless, there is often pressure from the students themselves to do just this. Progress is accounted in the measurable number of concepts covered, not their comprehension and application. Many bad bridge players adopt so-called scientific (hard) bidding systems in the hope that memorizing rules will make up for lack of natural ability. Unfortunately, their lack of 'feel' for the cards — a soft concept difficult to explain but easy to recognize — renders all such efforts of little account.

A large part of course design is making decisions about dependency. Do people need to know the inner workings of computers in order to learn systems analysis? Is a knowledge of double-entry bookkeeping necessary to understanding management ratios? If you ignore such dependencies you are asking people to take certain things on trust, which some people dislike; if you recognize them, and include the additional material, students may complain that the lecturer went into too much detail. Different students may have differing views of the dependencies resulting in both types of reaction on the same course!

Examining different teaching situations for dependency can provoke interesting alternatives to conventional teaching sequences. My view is that the main obstacle to learning to swim is fear of putting one's head under water. Most approaches to teaching swimming bend over backwards to avoid this happening in the early stages. This is sensible with children because the correct sequence is one of confidence-building. But with adults an approach that starts by persuading them to hold their breath and put their head under water for a very short time at first, then gradually increasing, would show faster results. It is much easier to learn to swim, if one is not struggling to keep one's head out of the water all the time.

Top-down

A principle that holds good for almost any communication is that of giving an overview before getting into detail — of going from the general to the specific. It is an essential teaching technique to put things in a wider context. People can then see relationships between apparently disconnected events or concepts, or the reasons behind the ways in which things are done, and are therefore more disposed to accept them, more likely to remember them — or sufficiently well informed to make constructive criticism.

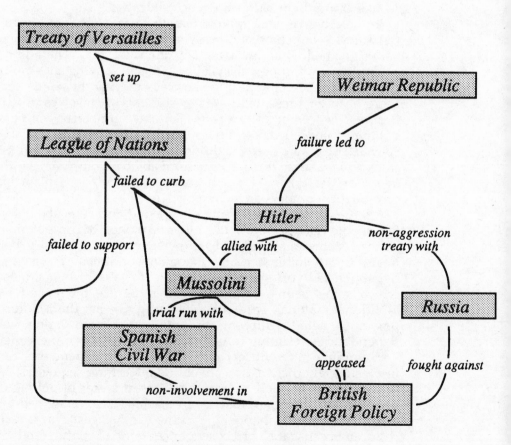

Figure 6.1 European history — relationship diagram

It is surprising how often opportunities for a top-down explanation are overlooked. I noted earlier that history is taught in a chronological sequence. This is not strictly true as it would imply that you were taught everything that happened in 1925 before you progressed to 1926. In reality what happens is that the subject is 'chunked' into major topics, which in many instances run concurrently, and then taught chronologically within these chunks. A better approach is to start with a top-down view (see Figure 6.1).

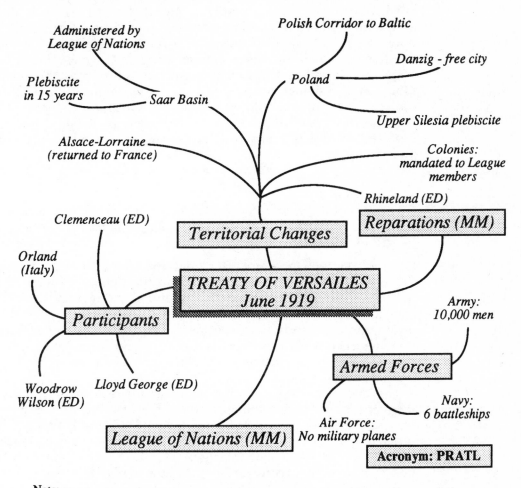

Note:
The MM entries refer to other Memory Maps which will be developed later in the course (thereby avoiding recording the same information twice). ED stands for Event Dictionary. This contains narrative entries for events, people or organisations not sufficiently important to merit a Memory Map but too important to leave at the level of an individual entry. PRATL is an acronym formed from the first letters of the headings. It is a memory aid (See Chapter 9).

Figure 6.2   Versailles Treaty — memory map

Figure 6.1 maps the relationships between the leading personalities and organizations of a period in history. As will be seen in more depth in Chapter 8, much communication is about identifying relationships. The Treaty of Versailles 'set up' the Weimar Republic and the League of Nations. The League of Nations failed to act against Hitler or to intervene in the Spanish Civil War. In this diagram the type of relationships are up to the teacher to define; with other material there may be a limited number of defined permissible relationships. An overview of this type gives students an immediate feel for the interdependence of historical events. It thus increases understanding. It also increases retention since long-term memory is based on association of ideas. The principle of top-down need not embrace only one level of breakdown. The top-level diagram can be 'decomposed' into as many lower level ones as required. Thus the Versailles Peace Treaty can be taken from the relationship model and a similar process applied — see Figure 6.2. This diagram replaces linear note-taking by a structure which more clearly shows the breakdown into successive levels of detail. By being a more logical representation it is easier for the student to assimilate and retain the information.

Teach, then do

C-l-e-a-n, clean, verb active, to make bright, to scour. W-i-n, win, d-e-r, der, winder, a casement. When the boy knows this out of the book, he goes and does it. Nicholas Nickleby, Charles Dickens

Dickens's Dr Squeers is not often held up as a model of good educational practice which is perhaps surprising in the light of general agreement that an ounce of doing is worth a pound of instruction. 'Doing' in this context may mean anything from school homework to a short exercise or lengthy case study on a commercial course. However articulate and clear we each think ourselves to be, we never know whether we have successfully communicated techniques or ideas until we have seen people applying them.

The classic example of this is in language teaching, whether the language is Arabic or BASIC. It is vital that, as soon as possible, people try out their newly-acquired knowledge. Teaching languages hard, in order to get students through exams, is a dependency sequence — you need to know nouns and their gender before you can learn adjectives; you cannot learn adverbs until you know verbs.

The learn-by-doing approach is to master a few sentences first within a defined environment, such as telling the time or shopping, and then immediately try them out. This is first and foremost a confidence-building approach derived from an analysis that identifies the basic problem with learning languages as unwillingness to 'have a go'. In teaching languages we can identify a basic 'survival kit' which will enable people to make themselves understood very quickly. The most useful thing to know, by far, are numbers. This enables people to buy things, tell the time and understand many common conversational topics. These can be followed by essential words enabling people to ask things — where, when etc. — and then concentration on the most common situations and talking points — weather, camp-sites, personal details, etc. This approach can equally well be categorized as a motivational one. Students are motivated by making observable progress in the subject and want to get on even faster.

When teaching computer programming I used to see just how little I needed to teach people before they wrote their first program. Far better to let them feel motivated by the success of seeing a program run — even if all it does is to take in some input and immediately print it out. All subsequent exercises then consolidate and extend this first piece of learning. A good metaphor is that of a snowball. By correctly identifying the basics of the topic we get people moving. Subsequent learning will reinforce previous lessons and add to it.

Do, then teach

The sequence 'teach, then do' is obligatory when students are being introduced to material or techniques of which they have no prior knowledge. However, much education and all coaching starts from the presumption of some familiarity on the part of the student. In this situation we may well wish to assess the student's ability before we start teaching or force our class to think for itself before influencing them with our ideas. When running a 'Training the Trainers' course, the first thing I do is to get the students to set up the training room. There is no one right way to set up a training room; it depends on the size of class, size and shape of room, type of training and instructor's own preference. Nevertheless, if I save this exercise until we are into the course, students will naturally tend to adopt that with which they have become familiar.

Only by doing it right at the beginning of the course (starting from stacked tables) can they be forced to make their own decisions. In addition, lugging tables around people setting-up video equipment and overhead projectors is a highly effective way of breaking the ice (not to mention your leg!).

In some situations we can use this sequence to add interest and therefore motivation. Postponing grammar until after the student has grasped some use of a language is an example. Teaching grammar first can be demotivational in that people become worried about making grammatical mistakes in speech and therefore are reluctant to speak. If we can motivate them by success in making themselves understood they will actively want to learn grammar as a means of extending their command of the language.

The above sequences, as stated earlier, can be applied at both the course and session level. When you get to the session level it becomes less easy to generalize about sequences as more depends on the subject being taught. Those that follow are the most commonly used.

Problem to solution

An example quoted earlier identified a sequence extremely common in the press and television — start with the most interesting bit. This sequence is mostly applicable at the session level. The idea of putting all the best bits of a course into the first day (and its going downhill from there) is not recommended!

Motivation is a vital part of training and there will often be times when people have been told to come, partly against their will, and they will need to be motivated before they can be taught anything.

Many teaching sessions have a disguised selling element. If we are giving a session on safety standards at work, we are not just describing the standards, we are trying to motivate people to adhere to them. We therefore need to adopt one of the techniques of selling which is to evoke a need, persuade people of the existence of a problem as a prerequisite of convincing them of our solution. If we fail in the persuasive part of such a training exercise we risk a zero transfer of the instructional part from classroom to workplace.

Similarly, on soft courses, we are often attempting to convince people of some cause and effect relationship — for example, that failure to delegate leads to bad decisions. In these cases, too, we will often choose to start with establishing agreement on the definition of the problem — bad decisions — before leading people to our solution.

Familiar to unfamiliar

Common to most sequences is the notion of increasing complexity. You start with relatively simple or familiar concepts and build on these. It is another form of dependency teaching. If people cannot grasp the basics it is not much use teaching them anything advanced. When we use analogies to explain new ideas we are building on what people already know. However, a characteristic of soft subjects (such as teaching) is that you can always find a contra-example to any all-embracing rule. One of the principles of so-called accelerated learning in teaching languages is that lessons do not get more difficult as you progress. Early lessons employ the full range of grammatical concepts so that the reward for progress is not to have something harder thrown at you. This, of course, is how we learn our own language.

Explain the purpose

An exercise I occasionally use is to ask someone to explain, in ten minutes, how to play chess. Almost invariably the explanation starts with the set-up of the board and then goes on to describe the different pieces and the moves they can make. The audience is asked to remember that pawns move one place ahead — although their first move may, or may not, be two places (also they capture diagonally); rooks move horizontally, bishops diagonally, the queen diagonally and horizontally — as can the king but only one square at a time — and knights move in an L-shape and are unique in that they alone can jump over intervening pieces. By now, confusion reigns. If the presenter is a chess enthusiast he is probably quite oblivious to this. To him it all seems very simple. Next the opening moves are discussed with some opaque advice about control of the centre of the board. Finally, we are introduced to the notion of 'check' and, with thirty seconds left, to 'checkmate'.

I refer to this type of teaching as the *suspension of comprehension*. Students are asked to remember a lot of new information, with the promise that 'everything will become clear in a minute'. Alas, it rarely does. The presenter has, without thinking, used a chronological sequence. He has described the game in the sequence in which it is played. This seldom works when explaining games. The better way is to start from the object or purpose of the game, i.e., to checkmate your opponent. Until someone has grasped the concept of checkmate he cannot understand anything about the game. He could perhaps answer a test about what pieces move in which direction and where they start on the board, but his grasp of the game would be zero. To explain chess you need to start with the simplest possible example of a checkmate, ensure that that is grasped (by inviting feedback) and then work backwards introducing the different pieces one at a time.

First things first

No one ever learns everything there is to know about anything but the most trivial subject. There is therefore always some element of prioritization in sequences as well as time location. Suppose we are running evening classes in first aid. We know from past experience that 40 per cent of the students will drop out in the course of the year. How do we decide what to teach first?

Clearly we shall start with any basics that are of the broadest relevance — pulse rate, breathing, etc. That done, we would then have a near-random list of ailments, accidents and so on that we wish to address. In the absence of any other criteria we would surely teach them in the order of probability of their happening. In Britain it makes sense to teach what to do in a traffic accident before how to treat heat exhaustion, and how to treat someone who has had an electric shock before administering to a snake bite. If time constraints on a session mean that we are not able to cover all the points we wish, we should put the most important first and make sure that all points are in the handouts.

Not all the above sequences are mutually exclusive. A course will often have a hierarchy with one overall sequence combined with different sequences for the individual sessions. The course may start with a top-down view of the subject matter and then follow a chronological sequence. Within this there may be dependent material requiring tests, and other practical work based on reinforcement of techniques just taught or anticipation of topics about to be covered.

Applying our own analysis, is course sequencing subject-dependent, environment-dependent or person-dependent? The sequence is dictated by the subject matter where what is being taught has a high level of dependency. This forces course designers into following a broadly similar sequence. It is environment-dependent in that class size, availability of time and equipment can significantly affect sequence. Where time is limited the presenter may have to 'teach, then do' rather than employ the lengthier approach of 'do, then teach'. It is person-dependent in as much as individuals — both teachers and students — have preferences. As a general rule, the more experienced people are, the more positively they react to an approach that puts doing before teaching or even leaves them to form their own conclusions. The less confident, the more people like courses to have a visible structure — to be told what to do first, rather than be thrown in at the deep end.

Link the sessions

The designer has now defined the sessions and specified the sequence in which they will be presented. It remains to make sure that they run logically together and fit conveniently within the course timetable. The latter may dictate another important sequencing decision — that of making post-lunch sessions participative. In similar vein he may choose to finish the day with practical work on the grounds that people may be content to stay later if they are absorbed in a problem — another device for squeezing more in. He may wish to alternate passive and participative sessions. Once these decisions have been taken they can be documented (and made convenient for review) in the macro-design form shown in Figure 6.3.

Macro Design Form

	Session title	Teaching points	Teaching method	Estimated time req.	Timetable	Sequencing	Est. dev. time
1	Room set-up and introduction	To teach, and give practice in, setting up a training room. To introduce course participants.	CE/L	2	1/18.00–20.00	1. Icebreaker 2. To teach room set-up without giving them preconceived ideas.	12
2	Individual presentations	To give practice in presentations and opportunity for filming and critique.	IP	4*	2/08.30–10.30 2/10.45–12.45	1. To evaluate individual student's ability 2. To give examples for subsequent discussion 3. To allow for review during the course	2
3	How to specify course	(1) To teach the theory of hard/soft and of teaching circles	L/Q	2	2/14.00–15.30 2/15.50–16.20	Lecture precedes exercise in order to teach them the theory of the method.	18
4	How to specify course	(2) To give practice in the theory.	SE SP	3 1.5	2/16.30–19.30 3/08.45–10.15	Practice in new theory	6
5	How to design a course	How to break a syllabus into teaching sessions. How to sequence the sessions. How to get a mix of teaching methods.	L SE SP	.25 6	3/10.15–10.30 3/10.45–13.00 3/14.00–18.30	Exercise precedes analysis—do, then teach	24
6	How to write a course (1)	Choosing the right medium, one way/two way; hard copy/ephemeral. How to write student handouts.	L/CE	1.5	4/09.00–10.30	Teach, then do	12
7	How to write a course (2)	The use of exercises/case studies writing hard/soft designing and producing visuals.	L	2	4/10.45–12.45	Teach, then do	18
8	How to write a course (3)	Practice in researching material and writing the training session.	SE	4	4/14.00–18.30	Practising what they have learned	24
9	Film reviews	To give students feedback on their own presentation style.			(Run in parallel with Session 8)		
10	How to give a formal lecture	How to establish contact. Recognizing different learning styles. Recognizing different teaching styles. Common presentational problems.	L/Q	3	5/09.00–10.30 5/10.45–12.15	Teach, then do	24
11	How to give one-to-one training	How to prepare and present a demonstration/hands-on teaching.	F/D	1.5	5/14.00–15.30	Teach, then do	6
12	Session writing	Preparation of teaching session.	SE	4	5/15.40–19.30 5/09.00–10.30	Exercise to give practice in techniques	2
13	Session presentations	Presentation of class teaching sessions.	SP	3*	6/11.00–13.00 6/14.00–15.00		1
14	Course summary	Evaluation/wrap-up	L	0.5	6/15.00–15.30		3

Figure 6.3   Macro-design form

Key to teaching methods: Figure 6.3

	L	lecturing—both formal instruction and instructor-led discussion
	CE	class exercise
	SE	syndicate exercise
*	GS	game/simulation
*	CS	case study
*	IP	individual presentations
	SP	syndicate presentations
	Q	questionnaire
	F	film
	D	demonstration by instructor
*	V	visit
*	CBT	computer-based training
*	PI	programmed instruction
*	IV	inter-active video
*		dependent on number of students

7

Session planning

Macro-design has given us a set of mini-specifications for sessions. It has made assumptions about how the sessions will be taught, partly in order to be able to apportion time between sessions. As we move into more detail we are guided by this but the session writer should still retain freedom, with consultation, to modify the session specification. In this we follow the principle that each phase anticipates its successor and can modify the output of its predecessor.

In planning a session the writer will first consider the sources of his material. Next he will plan the mix of teaching approaches that will be used. I use the word 'approach' to encompass the totality of methods, techniques and aids that the trainer employs. We can usefully divide these into two main categories:

- Training methods — lectures, group discussions, exercises, case studies. These are at the heart of session planning.
- Training aids — films, demonstrations, show and tell, computer-based training. These assist in the learning process either through adding variety or because in certain circumstances they are superior to lectures and exercises.

When planning a session I use the following checklist:

- What shall I *write* and they *read*?
- What shall I *say* and they *listen to* and *discuss*?
- What shall I *show* and they *watch*?
- What shall I *devise* for them to *do*?

These reflect two additional differences — between what is permanent and non-permanent, and between participative learning and passive learning. Neither difference is meant to embody a value judgement, although increasingly the tendency is for courses, in schools as well as commercial training, to become more participative and experiential. Both distinctions are further examples of a continuum rather than discrete sets. Reading a book or manual is mostly passive but participative

Experiencing Theory X Management

elements can be built in through questions and answers; lecturing can be purely one-way or can be an instructor-led discussion. The teaching methods grid shown in Figure 7.1 represents these variables as though they are discrete. The various teaching approaches have been plotted against the axes of passive-participative, permanent/non-permanent.

	Non-permanent	Permanent
Passive	lectures demonstrations	handouts displays films and videos
Participative	'hands-on' exercises case studies simulations/games	questionnaires skills learning (e.g. typing) computer-based training interactive video

Figure 7.1   Teaching methods grid

The grid in Figure 7.1 is a checklist of options open to the session writer. An analysis of the options is useful in deciding which to incorporate in a given session:

1. *Variety* The first and most obvious point is that by choosing approaches from more than one quadrant the designer gives variety to the session or course. This assists learning; it also helps to take the pressure off the course presenter.
2. *Reinforcement* The use of the word 'non-permanent' is deliberate. Without some form of permanent back-up, how much will the student remember six months after the course? If non-permanent methods are not hardened up by documenting the teaching points of the various exercises, such training experiences can be enormous fun, receive rave reviews and have little lasting effect.
3. *Timing* There is a trade-off between participation and timetable control. With no audience participation we can accurately predict the length of time a session will require. Once learning becomes participative, the time taken depends on the amount of interaction. This may, in turn, depend upon the number of students and their aptitudes and attitudes.
4. *Teaching strategy* Our choice of methods relates back to the teaching strategy grid in Chapter 2. Are we giving an overview of the subject — in which case a less participative approach may be needed — or are we teaching mastery of a technique or trying to change ingrained attitudes, both of which dictate a high level of audience participation?

Let us examine the different approaches and relate them to session planning.

Passive/Non-permanent

Lectures

It is important to define 'lecturing' as verbal interaction between a presenter and his audience, not a monologue. If there is no interaction a lecture is the wrong choice of medium. We would be better writing the information in a handout or, in certain circumstances, making a film or slide show. The proportion of speaking done by each party to the interaction will vary as a function of the material being covered. If the session is covering hard material, new to the audience, the lecturer will do most of the talking; if it is soft, the audience contribution will increase. In assigning part or all of a session to lecturing the designer will be thinking in terms of supporting visuals as well as lecture notes. Both these are at the heart of all courses and are covered in detail in the next section of this book.

Demonstrations

Demonstrations can range from a sample document or product specimen to a half-day visit to a computer installation or shop floor. They can be passive or participative. The question of sequence again arises. A visit can be a means of stimulating interest before introducing a new topic or it can be placed after, to act as reinforcement. Where the subject matter is complex I usually prefer to place visits after the relevant sessions. If the subject matter is relatively straightforward, a visit or demonstration can precede the teaching. It is more likely for demonstrations to go wrong than a classroom lecture session. They therefore require as much preparation as other aspects of the course.

Demonstrations can go wrong

Passive/Permanent

Handouts

I choose the term 'handouts' to include any form of written text, student manual, book, or operating manual, given to the delegate and which he is expected to retain and use after the course.

The trend towards participative learning suggests that two-way communication is superior to one-way in all respects and at all times. Not so. The written word is portable, reproducible and self-pacing. A student can turn back to verify a point that he missed. He can refer to it at any time in the future. Checklists survive long after discussions are forgotten. The teaching methods grid should not be interpreted as saying that soft subjects do not require hard copy. Even when we are teaching questions not answers, we still need people to remember the questions.

Passive/Permanent

The course designer must have a view about the function of the course handouts and how they are integrated with participative sessions. Are they:

- A security blanket, to save students the trouble of detailed note-taking?
- An authoritative and invaluable work of reference for use after the course?
- Something that students subsequently put under the leg of their desk to stop it from wobbling?

The important point is this. Course handouts are complementary to the lectures, not a transcript of them. The printed word is permanent, one-way communication. If there are 12 rules for some activity, write them in the manual and draw the students' attention to them. Rules are hard; they need no further explanation (though they may need practice in order to master their application). If the rules are complex, illustrate them with a worked example. If, however, they are only guidelines, then you need to discuss them. The difference between rules and guidelines is

65

that the latter are environment- or person-dependent. A discussion is therefore helpful in exploring what degree of universality they command and the circumstances in which they can be disregarded.

A student once remarked to me: 'You're like many lecturers, Colin. We're three-quarters of the way through the course and a third of the way through the manual.' At the time this caused me some embarrassment as I anticipated the feverish rush through the last 60 pages. Now I adopt the opposite approach. At the outset I make clear that some topics will not be covered in the lectures *because they are in the manual*. Using the manual to extend the area covered by the course is one way of getting a quart into a pint pot.

Displays

Another way of increasing the coverage of a course, and thereby adding value, is to have ancillary material to hand. My 'Training the Trainers' course has a book display of some 30 titles. In a session on visual aids I cannot hope to cover all the advanced effects that can be achieved, nor are most of my students likely to be interested. But if anyone is, there is a book available which gives more detailed information and techniques. In planning a session we should give thought to back-up material that can add interest and depth to the course. Such material can often help the presenter out of an awkward spot when he gets a question to which he does not know the answer. The display material could well have it.

Films and videos

I cannot deny that most of my students prefer watching a John Cleese training film to listening to me. Many commercial training films are so good that there is a real danger that the presenter who makes use of them finds his role diminished to that of projectionist. If this is not to happen, he must have decided well in advance how he is going to use the film, how he will build on it rather than be secondary to it. Since the film is going to beat him hands down as a one-way communication, it is up to him to maximize his advantage, namely that of two-way communication.

The following guidelines should govern the use of films and videos in training.

1. *Use only training films of the highest quality.* Current technology puts the potential for film-making and distribution within the reach of many more companies. I recently bought three one-hour cassettes on various aspects of information technology, total price under £50 (as against a price of around £500 each for equivalent films from a top film-making company). The reason for their cheapness rapidly became clear. The films' production costs had very obviously been underwritten by two or three companies whose products were heavily featured throughout.

2. *Plan how you will integrate the film into your session.* As with demonstrations we need to consider sequence. Is the film best shown at the start of the relevant session, as an introduction, or at the end for reinforcement? Used as an introduction a film can be referred back to by the lecturer, it can give a practical example to which he can relate the lectures. I have seen the Melrose Productions film *The Time Bomb* (about computer security) very effectively used in this way over a period of two days on a course on auditing computer systems. An advantage of finishing with a film is that the session will end on a high note. People can continue discussing the film over coffee or lunch.

3. *Use films to reinforce the message.* A technique I have occasionally adopted is to put a film on first thing in the morning following the day in which the material has been covered. This form of repetition is of proven benefit in increasing retention of the material. It is also another way to overcome the stragglers' syndrome. This is a useful approach in parts of the world where timekeeping is an imperfect discipline or where people are reluctant to admit ignorance for fear of losing face. The repetition in using the film gives them a non-threatening opportunity to catch up on anything they did not understand first time.

4. *Use videos to encourage participation.* Most films are designed to be projected remotely and are difficult to interrupt. Videos are far more flexible. The presenter can easily stop them and start a discussion. Many videos — particularly those concerning soft subjects — are specifically designed to make this happen. They have built-in 'break points' for class discussions. Usually there will be a presenter's guide which will give hints on how to lead such a session.

Participative/Non-permanent

Hands-on

I use the term 'hands-on' to designate hard/soft teaching where we are giving the student a taste of what a particular machine or instrument can do. Acquiring mastery comes under skills learning.

With a demonstration, the instructor, or a competent assistant, is explaining what one is seeing and, where necessary, pressing the buttons. Thus, providing it has been properly planned, things should remain under control. Restriction of interaction means events can be foreseen. A 'hands-on', i.e., allowing a student to press the buttons, is inherently more risky. I look at how to minimize the risk in Chapter 9.

Exercises/case studies/simulations/games

'Hands-on' implies the use of some form of machinery. Exercises may require no such props and are an opportunity to apply participative

67

techniques in any field of training. They can range from a short class test to a case study lasting for a complete course. They should form the heart of any course with a significant training or coaching content. Most course enhancement that I undertake revolves around the substitution of exercises for lecturing. The writing of exercises is covered in detail in Chapters 9 and 10 on hard and soft writing; case studies are dealt with as a separate topic in Chapter 11.

Participative/Permanent

Questionnaires

Questionnaires — as exemplified by the learning styles test in Chapter 5 — are a device for hardening up soft topics. Typically their designers have identified a number of characteristics — usually not greater than four — which are relevant to a particular discipline. They then devise a series of questions to test for the presence or absence of these characteristics and provide an analysis of strengths and weaknesses based on the individual's scores. They are most used in interpersonal skills courses. They can be a useful teaching aid though the presenter must agree with the relevance of the analysis. Like all such devices, a questionnaire should never be introduced merely to give variety — or to give the presenter a break!

Skills learning

This encompasses any activity in which we wish the student to gain mastery in some neuro-muscular skill. It is based on the ready availability of the necessary machinery and the design task is to specify a series of carefully graded practice exercises enabling the students individually to progress as fast as possible.

Computer-based training (CBT)

To what extent does CBT overcome the non-interactive nature of films? Clearly it is a participative medium, although only within the limits imposed by the computer program. CBT is a generic term covering among other things CMI (computer-managed instruction) where the computer manages the teaching in the sense of setting tests and routeing the student through different modules based on the results, and CAL (computer-assisted learning) which is the actual teaching programs. It is CAL that I shall now describe.

For a trainer to put CAL into its right place as a training aid it is helpful to understand a little of how it works. When an author writes a CAL program he essentially creates a number of screens, sometimes called frames. It is these that the student sees when the program is run. Each frame can contain text, including questions, and graphics. Sound is also available, though usually sound effects rather than synthesized speech. Thus in using the medium in 'book' mode the author can impart whatever information he wishes. Graphic effects can be created — for instance, to show two chemicals being mixed together — so that, without interaction, we already have a significant advantage over the written word.

But the basis of CAL is interaction. The computer poses a question and checks the student's answer. It can therefore be used for 'drilling' in subjects such as French verbs, arithmetic and historical dates. The common characteristic of these three is that they are all hard subjects. They all have precise right answers. With arithmetic or history we have the option to go one step further and check for a near answer. This is much easier when the input is numeric and we can set a 'close' range.

However, this becomes considerably more difficult to do if the input is alphabetic in response to an open question such as 'Which is the highest mountain in the world?' Not only are there near answers, which in this case means minor misspellings, there are multiple forms of the right answer. 'Mount Everest', 'Mt Everest' and 'Everest' are all correct.

The problem the computer has, which the human marker does not, is that its only means of recognizing right or wrong answers is by comparing the student's answer, character by character, with its own. In the case of the French verbs this is fine because it is the correct spelling that is being tested. But with Mount Everest we are testing geography, not orthography. And there are too many variants on the right answer for the author to be able to code every one into the program.

The simplest way round this problem is to restrict the student's freedom of answer by using multiple-choice questions. By definition then the only permissible responses are the numbers or letters that define the choices. This is excellent for the computer but less so for the students since it entails showing students the right answer, albeit among a selection. This is why such systems, much used in non-computer-based examinations, are referred to by schoolchildren as 'multiple-guess'.

Having said this, there are undoubted advantages of CAL over human instructors. Among these we can itemize:

- The computer does not tire, nor does it get out of bed on the wrong side.
- The graphic facilities of the computer are invaluable. I have used them to help with keyboard familiarization; airlines, slightly more ambitiously, use them to simulate Jumbo jets.
- It is self-pacing.
- It is suitable for distance-learning.
- The quality of instruction is uniform.
- All students work through precisely the same material.

It is important for the professional trainer to be aware of the situations in which CAL can be used to advantage. The underlying technology makes it highly applicable to subjects with a high 'T' content. The hardness of the material, allied with the need to give students practice in mastering techniques through drill or structured exercises, means that CAL can act as a 'stand-alone' teaching medium.

Interactive video

It is instructive to see how an intrinsically hard medium comes to terms with soft subjects. One avenue is by merging the different technologies of CBT and films. In this way a student can be shown a filmed situation displayed on a computer screen and then asked questions about it. It is possible to simulate, for example, a sales situation and then ask the student why the salesman failed to close. Considerable improvements in the quality of such programs have been made in the last few years. Nevertheless, in this type of situation, the computer is still more a training aid than a stand-alone device.

A worked example

Figure 7.2 shows detailed session plans for a 'Training the Trainers' course:

Session 6 How to write a course

Time	Content	Sources	Visuals	Student handouts	Presenter's guide	Equipment required	Development time Estimated	Actual
15 min	Explanation of teaching methods grid	THTS	Teaching Methods Grid	THTS	THTS		2	
45 min	Six tables exercise	Games Trainers Play	Two diagrams	Analysis of solution	Instructions on how to run exercise		5	

Session 10/11 One-to-one: How to give a formal lecture

Time	Content	Sources	Visuals	Student handouts	Lecturer notes	Equipment required	Development time Estimated	Actual
30 min	You'll soon get the hang of it	Video arts	None	Briefcase booklet	Briefcase booklet	Video/TV	1	
30 min	How to give a demonstration	THTS	BASIC/COBOL	Guidelines for demonstrations	Instructions for running demo	PC	6	
15 min	Establishing class contact	THTS	Guidelines	Annotated guidelines	None		2	
30 min	Learning styles questionnaire (LSQ)	Honey and Mumford	Blank LSQ grid LSQ scores by type of job	LSQ questionnaire analysis of scores	LSQ book		2	
30 min	Common presentational problems	KLA ICS course	Cartoons from THTS	Illustrated faults and difficult students	Refer KLA joke book nos 124–136		4	

Figure 7.2   Session plans

Part III
Writing the course

The output from design — validated by a review — is a set of session plans. The sessions now have to be written. I use 'writing' in a wide sense to include the adaptation of existing courseware to fit into a new course. Session writing, in part or whole, may be done by the course designer. Alternatively, individual sessions may be contracted out to a number of different people. In the latter situation, session planning is particularly useful for the designer since he is able to give a detailed specification to writers who may not be professional course developers.

What and how we write depends upon the characteristics of the material and the audience. Writing will almost invariably involve some research. Even when the course writer is an expert in the subject matter he will still usually need to go back to some original material to assist him in defining procedures and describing skills that he now uses without any need for thought. We can divide such research into:

1. Published material

    * Legal documents, e.g. Sale of Goods Act
    * Company standards, e.g. contracts of employment
    * Operating manuals
    * Books.

2. Original research.
    Where the course writer is reliant on his own expertise, or that of others, to define the skills that require teaching.

Research, whether reading or discussion, is one of the most stress-free activities in any form of writing. All the difficulties arise when you have to convert research into a manual, paper or lecture. Now it is necessary to be creative as well as analytical. Writing is a soft activity; different people do it in different ways. The only guidelines I can offer — beyond those in the next four Chapters — are:

* Accept that all creative work is iterative by nature — you will not get it right first time.
* Consult widely with others on all aspects of research and development of material.
* Pay attention to your working environment; most of us have a time, place and manner of working that is more productive than others.

8
Clarifying the material

To write effective training material you must:

- Understand the topic clearly yourself.
- Be able to communicate this understanding to others.

Understanding the topic

This appears self-evident. But above I inserted the adverb 'clearly'. There's the rub. I used to run courses on effective writing. The expectation, or hope, of many delegates on the course was that I would wave a magic wand over their head which would turn their laboured prose into models of clarity — that I possessed the philosopher's stone of writing. Alas, I had to disappoint them. For the most part their problem was not an inability to write clearly, it was an inability to think clearly. One of the basic principles of selling is 'First convince yourself'. We can modify this for teaching to say, 'Before explaining things to others, explain them to yourself'.

It is my contention that clear thinking is largely a matter of accurate perception of the relationships between the parts that constitute the whole. The commonest relationships that we encounter are itemized below.

From premise to conclusion

The relationship here is the logical flow from an accepted premise to a hitherto unfamiliar conclusion, which then becomes the new knowledge. With hard subjects one can finish with the letters QED to show that it is a correct proof. With hard techniques you can see the proof in the working model that has just been constructed.

In soft subjects there is no equivalent measure of proof. Can I prove that delegation is central to good management? In what sense do I personally 'understand' how to develop courses? The only evidence is that I have written this book. But that is poor stuff compared to the logical proof of Pythagoras' theorem or the evidence of your eyes of a financial model that I have just constructed. The last word has been said about right-angled triangles but after 20 years I am still learning about course development.

In the soft situation the writer has to persuade his audience that the ideas put forward are valid. There are a number of common ploys that are employed:

1. He can explain the theory behind the method or solution he is putting forward and hope that people will agree with his conclusions by agreeing his premises and the intervening steps.
2. He can appeal to a higher authority by quoting the findings of a recognized expert in the field.
3. He can cite examples — a common lecturing technique. But often examples can be found which prove the opposite.
4. He can quote statistics — which are merely a collation of a larger number of examples. In my field of lecturing (systems development) there was a graph published many years ago which showed, in a strictly limited area, that modifications made to systems during the development process became exponentially more expensive the further through the project one had got. This graph has been reproduced probably more than any other single statistic in the computer industry as authoritative support for what everyone feels to be obvious but no one can prove.

Discrete sets

If we are writing a course about legislation that affects people's personal or working life it is likely that we will be helped by the propensity of the law to put things into watertight categories. The law has to lay down unambiguous — 'hard and fast' — rules about, for example, entitlement to benefits. It cannot leave decisions regarding eligibility to the discretion of individual social security clerks. Consequently, the law deals in distinct sets of people defined by variables such as sex or age. (The latter continuous variable is made discrete by setting defined points such as age 65.) Thus on this topic the course writer has only to explain the rules. There should be no room for doubt about categories — no lengthy discussion about what it means to be male or female, above or below sixty-five.

Diffuse sets

The significance of the above can be seen by reference to the situation where there is room for interpretation. Suppose entitlement to benefit were determined by 'perceived need'. We have substituted a relative concept for an absolute. Immediately, different people can hold contrasting views. In place of clear categories the course writer now has to deal in guidelines, limits of discretionary action, appeals procedures and the like. He has to adjudicate cases put to him by his students — at the risk of subsequently being overruled. The teaching has switched from subject-dependent to environment- and person-dependent, (the claimants' circumstances are subjectively assessed by the decision-maker).

Arranging things in logical sets is a prerequisite of clear communication. For example it forces us to think whether the definition of a spreadsheet includes any reference to computers or 'software' or whether a piece of paper can be a spreadsheet. If 'software' is not its set, what is? The question is not academic. Putting things into sets is a most powerful form of shorthand — always providing that the two parties are both familiar with the set in question. Defining something as a 'vehicle' immediately suggests wheels, some form of locomotive power, steering and so on.

In many instances the writer will search in vain for clear definitions to help him — particularly if he ventures into political science (a misnomer if ever there was one) or religion. What nuance of policy separates the Workers' Revolutionary Party from the Socialist Workers' Party, from militant tendency, from the Marxist league and so on? What is the definition of a Christian? Resolving problems such as these is how a good communicator imposes a structure on what he teaches.

Communicating to others

The above type of analysis is what any communicator has to do before he can think of beginning to write course material. It is particularly necessary for the expert who has been called in. His problem is an inability to see the wood for the trees. By standing back and examining what is being taught through the prism of set theory or as a logical progression from premise to conclusion, our chances of communicating our understanding to others are maximized. He will also have to 'shape' the material. This will mean asking:

- Where should I start from? How much knowledge can I assume my audience has?*
- How much do they need to know? (which can be related to the teaching strategy grid).
- Do I need to explain the 'why' and 'how' as well as the 'what'?

One of the best ways of looking at course writing is to consider the typical questions that come up in any teaching session. The most common classes of questions are:

*An axiom that has stood me in good stead throughout my lecturing career is: Never over-estimate an audience's knowledge; never under-estimate an audience's intelligence.

1. *Have I understood what you are saying?* These are questions of the sort: 'Are you saying that . . .?', 'Does that mean that if I did this, that would happen?' or 'Can *x* and *y* both be present at the same time?' With hard subjects this may be merely a request for clarification. With soft subjects it may go deeper. It may ask the teacher to define a relationship — that *b* is caused by *a*, or that *a* merely precedes *b*. It may look to see whether two terms are discrete or overlapping, for example 'Could you explain the exact difference between sales and marketing?'

2. *Do I accept what you are saying?* These are questions of the type: 'On what basis do you say . . .?' 'Acceptance' is a word most associated with soft teaching. We immediately see the use of statistics as a form of substantiation, if not proof. This is the most obvious way in which we could defend the proposition that 'seat belts save lives' or 'smoking causes cancer'. Consideration of this type of question forces the course writer into locating such supporting material. If it cannot be found then the proposition rests on nothing other than 'proof by repeated assertion'.

3. *How generally applicable is what you are saying?* Again, soft questions, of the type: 'Is that always the case?' Pythagoras' theorem is applicable universally (on a flat plane, that is!). Maslow's hierarchy of needs may work better in the United States than in the Far East.

4. *How much importance should I attach to this?* These often come in the form of questions about an event's probability of happening: 'How likely is it that both computers will go down at the same time?' or relevance to the student, 'Does it matter to me if . . . couldn't I do my job anyway?' An invaluable question to be asked during reviews, if the writer has not already asked it, is 'So what?' Directed at specific material it asks, in a very succinct way, what significance there is in the point being made and whether the students require this information.

Awareness of these typical classes of questions helps us to write material in such a way as to either anticipate them or deal with them when they arise. Broadly there are three methods of explaining:

- Explanation by definition
- Explanation by example
- Explanation by analogy.

Explanation by definition

An exercise that I use on my communication courses is to get students to define an 'owl'. Before doing so we first agree on the criteria for a good definition: someone who has never seen an owl should now be able to recognize one when he sees it. More than that, he should also be able to recognize non-owls. Definitions are a form of specification; they must exclude as well as include. To define anything you must start with the overall set to which it belongs; other members of this set are then excluded from the overall set by defining the differentiating characteristics. Thus an owl is placed in the set of 'birds' or, to be precise, a subset, 'birds of prey'. It is then distinguished from other members of the set, such as golden eagles, by characterizing it as nocturnal and going 'too-whit, too-whoo.*

OWL: A nocturnal bird of prey, with a wide face and large, forward-facing eyes, that emits a distinctive hooting sound

But what if the audience does not share the common base knowledge? It is no good describing an owl as a bird of prey to someone to whom the concept of 'bird' is meaningless. Explanations work by going from the familiar to the unfamiliar. They assume a common base of knowledge or experience. If this assumption is incorrect we get feedback of the form; 'I'm sorry, I don't understand what you mean by . . .'.

*An owl is deemed unlucky in some Arab countries. A definition supplied by a student in the Middle East was 'A bird with big eyes. If you see it you will have bad luck all day'. This rates as the nicest definition I have heard but it would not recommend itself to your average lexicographer.

When a common base is lacking we have to regress to find the point at which we both understand the same concept. If we are describing an owl to a Martian he may not recognize the concept 'bird'. We must go back one step:

Bird: a two-legged animal with feathers.

The trap to avoid here is to mention the word 'flying'. This would rule out a perfectly legitimate bird such as the emu. Again we see the process of placing it within its set and then giving it a distinguishing characteristic within that. If our Martian has led a particularly sheltered existence we may have to continue the regression:

Animal: a living thing that moves.

This should be enough because presumably he himself falls within this definition but if there is still a problem:

Thing: any object of knowledge or perception.

The exercise gets more difficult as you regress (and become more abstract), illustrating again that it is easier to communicate in specifics than abstractions.

The example extends our set theory of explanation into the notion of a hierarchy. This contribution to understanding is exactly what the

Swedish naturalist Karl von Linné made when he compiled his taxonomy of animals and plants. This classification is hard, only borderline cases such as plants that eat things posing any problems of interpretation.

Suppose you are asked to give a lecture about art. Someone in your audience pops up with the helpful comment that he does not consider a pile of bricks to be art just because the trustees of the Tate Gallery were daft enough to put it in an exhibition. Such a discussion could rapidly degenerate and run out of control. Few of us have not had the wind taken out of our lecturing sails at some time by someone questioning first principles. Before setting out on the lecture we need to be clear about our own definition of a work of art.

The ability to define things is very important, mainly because it forces us to get our own mind in order. However, it is not always the best way to explain complex issues, particularly if the thing to be explained is not obviously a member of a discrete set. For example, a question I have been asked many times is: What do computer people mean when they talk about a database? Much education is concerned with taking the mystique out of technical terms like this. Mystique convinces people that they cannot understand something which in reality is quite simple. How then do we explain a database? Explanation by definition gives us: 'Database: An integrated collection of interconnected records of many types that is organized according to a logical structure in which redundancy can be minimized'. Though this meets our criteria for a definition (a 'collection of records' is the set, the rest is the differentiation), I suspect that my audience would be little the wiser. Worse still, I would have confirmed their prejudice that computer people speak a mysterious language all their own. Explanation by definition is a commendably rigorous approach but it is not always the best way to make oneself understood.

Explanation by example

To explain what a database is I can give an example of one. I start from three conventional files, as shown in Figure 8.1, all based on employees — payroll, personnel records and training. I ask my audience whether they can see any problems caused by having three separate files all relating to essentially the same set of data.

You do not need to know anything about computers to see that there is a lot of duplication between the files and that, separately maintained, they could contain contradictory information about the same person. Once this problem is grasped I draw a simplified hierarchical representation of one file containing all the data and which can be used independently by the various departments as shown in Figure 8.2.

When lecturing I would get feedback to ensure that my audience understands the difference between the two types of files. Only then do I give the second one its technical name of a database. This sequence follows another rule — *explanation first, jargon second*. If you start from

Payroll	Personnel records	Training
Employee no.	Employee no.	Employee no.
Department	Department	Department
Salary	Address	Qualifications
Review date	Tel. no.	Date of joining
Tax code		
Deductions	Next of kin	Skills profile
YTD gross	Date of joining	Courses attended
YTD tax	Doctor	Courses planned
NI no.	....	....
....	....	....

Figure 8.1 Separate files

a statement 'I shall now explain what a database is', you are starting from the unfamiliar and you run a risk of 'turning people off'. If you start from a familiar concept of a filing system, then involve the audience in identifying the problems when three separate files store the same data, people see for themselves the problems that databases overcome. Typically they react with the comment 'Well there's nothing much to that, is

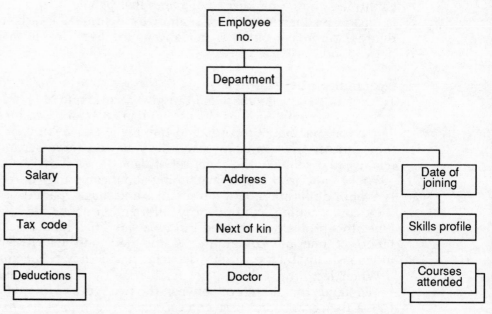

Figure 8.2 Representation of a data base file

there?' Far from considering this a put-down I value this as evidence of my success in simplifying the subject.

Explanation by example frequently makes clear what explanation by definition has confused. Indeed it is often explicitly asked for by students who are having trouble understanding: 'Can you give me an example of what you mean?'

Concepts, as opposed to facts, are always difficult to define. For example, it is almost impossible to give a definition of the concept of 'seven'. Consulting a dictionary will not be a great help: 'Seven: a number one greater than six'. Then, 'Six: a number one greater than five'. This form of definition continues until you reach one. Then you exit from the regression: 'One: single, a unity . . .' You search eagerly for 'single': 'Single: one only, not double . . .'. At the end you arrive at a circular definition, which is equivalent to saying that the term is indefinable.

How then can we communicate the concept of number? Clearly not by definition because of the circularity. The only solution is explanation by example — to show people examples of sets of seven items and hope that they finally grasp that what there is in common between seven fingers, seven pencils, seven pins and so on is their 'sevenness'. This may seem a rather philosophical point but it has much relevance in training. Examples are specific, intelligible and persuasive.

Explanation by analogy

A typical soft relationship between two objects is that one is in some way 'like' the other. Let me continue with my database example. There is a second concept that I want my audience to grasp. This is that a database gives us the ability to access the stored information in different ways. It is not immediately clear what I mean by this statement. I expand my explanation: we can print reports based on employee number, department, nationality, sex or any other characteristic that we determine at the time of setting up the file. When I present the course, I watch my

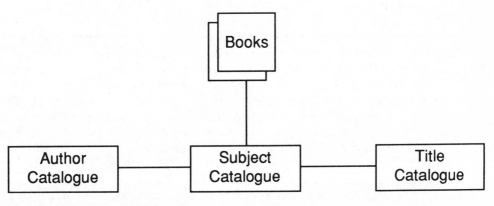

Figure 8.3   Library cataloguing system

audience's body language to see if they understand what I am saying. If they do not I need to find a different explanation. I draw them an analogy. (See Figure 8.3.)

An analogy can only be with something with which people are already familiar. Hence my choice of a library. A library is a centralized store of books arranged in one physical sequence (usually by subject since that is the most common requirement for retrieval). The library will have a subject catalogue enabling one to browse through a particular subject and find a relevant book. In addition to this there will be separate catalogues, by author and title so that people can locate a particular book when the title or author is the information they have about them. A database is similarly a set of records which users can access in different ways.

Let us go back to our dictionary in order to make the point more general. We look up the word 'blue'. We are given its set, 'a colour', but after that it is a bit difficult to find the words to differentiate blue from other members of the same set. (Not, admittedly, in a scientific dictionary, but that is a question of your audience.) My dictionary adds: 'like the colour of the sky'. Resisting the temptation to be sidetracked into discussions about the usual colour of the sky in England, what we again see is the process of explanation by analogy.

The colloquial way in which we ask people to describe things is to ask 'What's it like?' — 'What's Sydney like?' 'A bit like San Francisco without the fog'. This answer is tolerable provided, as always, that the questioner knows San Francisco.

The question: 'What is heaven like?' is much harder to answer. The trickiness of this question stems mainly from the fact that no one has come back to tell us. But it stems also from the absence of any commonly-agreed comparator. Religious fundamentalists have no problem in answering the question. They describe heaven in terms readily associable with terrestrial phenomena. It is those religions which take a softer, more spiritual, view of the matter that have all the problems. They are reduced to phrases such as, 'the presence of God'. This may, or may not, be good theology, but it is poor communication since it can mean all things to all men. By now this should come as no surprise. It is merely another example of how much more difficult it is to communicate soft than hard.

Which analogy people choose for the brain may affect their attitudes to learning. If you see it as a warehouse you may subconsciously feel that you ought not to clutter it up with too much information and that a periodic clear-out is required; if you see it as a muscle you would expect that the more you put it to use, the more powerful it becomes. One analogy leads to the conclusion that there is a finite amount of information you can remember at any one time; the other says that the more you remember, the more you will be able to remember.

Explanation by analogy is powerful both for hard and soft topics. Analogies are used not merely to explain, but as the basis of initiating action. In politics, people look to historical analogies to assist in the formulation of policy. In 1956 Britain invaded the Suez Canal Zone because the then prime minister, Sir Anthony Eden, saw an analogy between Nasser's annexation of the Suez Canal and Hitler's march into the Rhineland in 1936. Whether the analogy was accurate or not we have no means of knowing. Soft subjects such as politics do not allow controlled experiments.

9
Writing hard

The previous chapter looked at the various techniques for explaining points and for persuading people. Let us now discuss course writing. Within the set of hard courses we can distinguish between skills teaching and factual teaching. The former of these — double-entry bookkeeping, typing and so on — will be heavily dependent on practical work. The latter embraces all those areas in which we want people to remember specific facts after the course. Before looking at the techniques for achieving this we should first ask the question: Do we need people to remember information or is it sufficient that they have the information readily available?

The information explosion is producing ever more facts which become redundant at an ever-increasing rate. Today's working definition of an expert is not someone who knows all about a subject, but someone who knows where to go to find the answer. In many instances the latter is all we need to teach.

Writing lectures

Nevertheless, there are procedures, facts and rules that people have to remember. You will not get far in your driving test if, when asked about the Highway Code, you explain that you never bother to memorize anything that you can look up. Airline cabin crew have to know emergency procedures by heart. If ever I require mouth-to-mouth resuscitation I hope there is someone around who remembers what to do. Nor is it much good sending someone off to Paris with an English-French dictionary and the helpful comment that it contains all the words he needs. Salesmen who have to look up product information in a catalogue do not particularly impress prospective purchasers. Some information we need to fix in students' long-term memory. How do we accomplish this?

There are many excellent books, published recently, about the workings of the memory.* If we want our students to remember facts and

*For example, *The Brain Book*, Peter Russell, Routledge, Chapman & Hall.

"I know it's here somewhere....."

figures we should be aware of how best to make this happen. The techniques can be categorized as:

- Repetition
- Acronyms
- Alliteration
- Rhymes
- Meaningful illustrations.

Repetition

Most people can remember their own name, address and telephone number. They have seldom made a conscious effort to commit these to memory, it has come about through constant repetition. Presumably on courses we could make students write out a hundred times anything we wanted them to remember. But one has the instinctive feeling that this is likely to lead to a certain loss of motivation as well as suffering from the law of diminishing returns.

However, there is a serious case to be made for some form of repetition. It has been established that reviewing one's notes at the end of the day substantially improves retention. It is part of the process of fixing the material in long-term memory. I once tried an experiment on a course to validate this. The class had watched an interesting and informative talk on bee-keeping. That evening I asked two of the 12 class members to read once through copies I had made of the visuals used in the presentation. The next morning I sprang a surprise quiz on the class.

I must not change my mind after agreeing the specification

Learning by repetition

The two chosen students scored 18 and 19 (out of 20); the average of the other ten students was eleven.

Acronyms

An acronym is a word formed from the initial letters of other words. Gigo — garbage in, garbage out — is well-known in the computer industry as a warning against inaccurate data. Banks advise you to make an acronym of the letters equivalent to your personal identification number, another example of data that is better kept in your head than written down. Other examples abound. The following example is a set of guidelines for business letter writing:

Situation — explain the previous situation
Complication — what has gone wrong with it
Resolution — how to solve the problem
Action — what needs doing
Politeness — sign off.

Alliteration

Alliteration relies on the same sort of technique as acronyms. It is just that it is difficult to make up an acronym with only one letter at your disposal. The Video Arts film on sales presentations, 'Making Your Case', advocates the use of the four Ps:

*P*osition — state where you start from
*P*roblem — define what is wrong with the current position
*P*ossibilities — describe the various options available
*P*roposal — put forward the one you are recommending.

Rhymes

People studying anatomy remember the main nerves of the brain by the rhyme:

> On Old Olympus' Towering Top
> A Finn And German Viewed A Hop

This may not be great poetry, but it is very helpful in passing medical exams as a means of recalling the optic, olfactory, oculomotor, trochlear, trigeminal, abducent, facial, auditory, glossopharyngeal, vagus, accessory and hypoglossal nerves!

Meaningful illustrations

I once read an article about Jack Nicklaus's lifetime winnings on the American professional golf circuit. Significantly, I cannot recall the precise total. What I can remember though is that it was equivalent to 27 dollars for every stroke that he played. This immediately conjured up a mental picture of Nicklaus crouched over a 40-ft putt thinking to himself that it was worth $27 if he holed it, but $81 if he three-putted. By reducing a large figure to something within my compass the reporter had fixed it in my memory.

Enormously large figures seldom make for effective communication. Only a minuscule percentage of the population would know whether the UK national debt is £30 billion, £300 billion or £3000 billion. To communicate whatever figure it is we need to produce a comprehensible figure such as '£3000 for every man, woman and child in the United Kingdom'.

The general rule that this illustrates is: be specific. All good communicators — when they want to make themselves clear — speak in specifics. Notice how many newspaper articles start off with a specific instance or event before proceeding with the body of the story. Generalities send people to sleep; specifics keep them interested. This is why good lecturers illustrate what they are teaching with examples and anecdotes taken from real life.

Writing a lecture/demonstration

Central to all teaching is the ability to simplify. Suppose I asked you to summarize the Bible in 500 words. By now you know that the first thing you must ask is for me to define precisely the boundaries. I say that it is to include both Old and New Testament. I suspect your initial reaction would be that the task is near-impossible. Nevertheless, I insist. The question is 'What gets lost in the summarization?'

First, you have to completely disregard some books in their entirety. Presumably these will be those you judge to be the least important. Secondly, you are forced to leave out all qualifications. 'Thou shalt not kill' stays just that; if there is any caveat with respect to self-defence that is too bad. You have not got room to include it. Thirdly, any conflicting versions of events are ignored. The Gospels tell differing versions of the life and death of Jesus. Too bad. You will just have to pick on one and use that as the basis of your summary.

This is an example of the problem that faces anyone obliged to compress a broad and complex subject into a brief lecture. We cannot do the subject justice; in extreme cases we may even distort the truth, or at least give a partial or misleading view of it. How can we go about this in such a way as to give our audience the amount of information they require whilst minimizing the inaccuracies we have to commit to do this?

Let us switch topics. We have five minutes in which to explain a motor car to someone who has never seen one before. Of course, we would need to know just how much he does know that is related. Does he know what a wheel is, for example? Assuming a very basic knowledge of machinery we might divide our talk into five main topics:

- Power
- Transmission
- Electrics
- Steering
- Seating.

What we have done is to concentrate on the commonalities between the many different types of cars. What we ignore is the differences. We leave aside the fact that some cars are petrol-driven and some diesel; that some gearboxes are manual and others automatic. We can relate this ignoring of differences back to our theory of sets. We are effectively describing the determinants of the set called 'cars', whilst passing over the characteristics which differentiate one make of car from another.

In fact we have more than five minutes. We have 45 minutes and the lesson is to include a demonstration. Now things are different. Whereas our initial talk concentrated on cars in general, a demonstration is perforce on one car in particular. We therefore need to introduce things that are specific to this model of car. We are well-advised to do this before starting the demonstration. Whilst we are still in lecture mode we can restrict the number of new concepts that we introduce; we can pause to get feedback to make sure that people have understood. Immediately our audience catches a sight of the actual car they will see many things — aerial, windscreen wipers, radio, number plates — that are unimportant and extraneous. These will divert attention away from what we want them to concentrate on. By explaining the concepts before the demonstration we keep control. Our audience now knows what it is that we want them to see in the demonstration. We might even allow them a 'hands-on'!

From the above example we can derive a model of how to explain and demonstrate a complex subject when teaching hard/soft:

- Explain the concepts common to all instances of what one is teaching — cars, spreadsheets, generating stations.
- Explain the specific way in which these concepts are implemented in the example that we will be demonstrating.
- Give a demonstration, concentrating on the important concepts and rigorously refusing to be side-tracked.
- Let students practise for themselves on carefully graded exercises (*optional*).

On courses on computers I used to spend a session explaining what a program was; how it was written and what the problems were in subsequently modifying it. This was not because I expected my audience of senior managers to become programmers themselves; it was because there is a dependency between programming and systems (the latter being that in which they were most interested). If a manager has no appreciation of what a program is it is difficult to persuade him why he cannot keep changing his mind when specifying his requirements for a new system. Only when he has some appreciation of the problems caused by changing a program specification, will he seriously adhere to standards in developing systems. We are therefore teaching a hard subject in a soft way — getting over the broad concepts without worrying about the detail, giving them a feel for the subject, not trying to turn them into experts. Programming is a complicated business. The average programming reference manual runs to a couple of hundred pages. Let us get out Occam's razor.

William of Occam was a medieval
scholastic famous for reducing everything
to its barest essentials

1. *Reduce programming languages to their common elements*. All programming languages have five basic instructions only. They enable you to:

   ● Read data into the computer
   ● Do arithmetic on it
   ● Branch — that is to jump to an instruction other than the next in sequence
   ● Make a decision — based on comparing two values
   ● Print out the results.

2. *Show how these instructions are represented in a specific language*. I need here to make quite certain that my audience understands that this is one specific language that is fully representative of all others. Otherwise their technical people will undermine my teaching when they get back by pointing out that they do not use the language in question (BASIC).

   The instructions in BASIC are:

   ● Input
   ● Let A+B = C (Addition)
   ● Go to . . . (followed by the number of the instruction to which to jump)
   ● If A = B then . . .
   ● Print.

Alongside I write up the equivalent instructions in another programming language just to make sure they get the point made above.

I discuss this set of instructions whilst still in front of the class in order to make sure that my audience understands and to take any questions before I start the demonstration. I warn them to ignore some of the things which they will see when I turn the computer on 'Just house-keeping messages' and concentrate on the program that I will write for them.

3. *Give the demonstration.* The secret of any demonstration is *control.* The secret of control is *preparation.* The program I now write has been stripped to the very basics. I am dependency teaching because once anyone is lost they have had it. So I take it a step at a time. All the while I am subtly trying to undermine the mystique associated with computers. My audience's perception of a program is something very complex which takes ages to write and then cannot be touched. We will destroy that by the simple expedient of writing a program in ten seconds flat:

```
10   Input A ('A' stands for 'any number' — like the algebraic use
     of x and y)
20   Print A
```

Hey Presto — a program! Not a very ambitious one, I am forced to admit, but a program all the same. I run it and ask someone for a number to put in for 'A'. The computer obediently accepts the number and prints it out. Everyone still with me? Next instruction:

```
10   Input A
20   Print A
30   Let A = A+2
40   Print A
```

The third instruction has the effect of incrementing the value of 'A' by two. We run the program again and the computer prints out whatever value we put in for 'A' and then prints out a value two greater. Now we need to show the effect of a branch instruction:

```
10   Input A
20   Print A
30   Let A = A+2
40   Print A
50   Go to 30
```

Now the program always jumps from instruction 50 back to instruction 30. It is in a 'closed loop'. The effect is that the computer keeps adding two and printing the result until such time as I hit the 'Escape' key. We get out of the loop by inserting an instruction that will ultimately cause it to exit:

```
10   Input A
20   Print A
30   Let A = A+2
35   If A = 1000 then stop
40   Print A
50   Go to 30
```

This time *I choose* the value to be put in for 'A'. Why? Because I want to be sure that it is an even number. Since we have made the test 'A = 1000' an odd number value for A will not cause the program to exit from the loop. Of course I claim to be putting in 'any old number'. This piece of theatre is to enable me to ask the students whether they can see anything wrong in the program — which, given the judicious input of an even number, appears to be functioning perfectly. If they can then come up with the correct instruction:

35 if A > 1000 then stop

they are far more involved and motivated than if I had continued in 'telling' mode and given them the answer.

In writing this demonstration I am obeying a number of self-imposed rules:

- I keep the demonstration very simple. There is a useful guideline here: *the more complex the technique, the simpler the example.*
- I take it one step at a time — because a demonstration is almost always dependency teaching.
- I keep control by unobtrusively choosing when I ask the audience to contribute and when to keep things in my own hands

In this example we see, in practice, the point made in Chapter 4 that a well-written hard course is a long way down the road to success.

Writing exercises

The characteristic of hard exercises is that they have a correct solution (or multiple correct solutions). The main skill in writing them is in pitching them at the right level, not trying to teach too much simultaneously, and being willing to split a complex exercise into two or three simpler, graded ones.

Computer systems design

Some years ago I used to teach computer fundamentals to non-computer managers. Part of the course covered how systems are designed. This involved an explanation of files, inputs and outputs, all of which are sufficiently machine-dependent to be hard and sufficiently technical to be soporific. To counter the latter problem I devised the following exercise. It consists in taking a typical piece of computer-produced output — in this instance a gas bill (see Figure 9.1) — and identifying where the data necessary to produce the bill has come from.

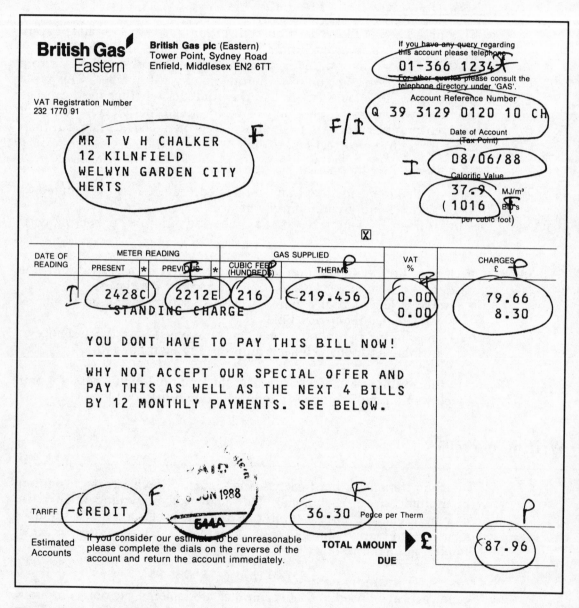

Figure 9.1 Gas Bill

I chose this particular output because everyone is familiar with public utility bills. I explain that everything printed on the bill has either to have come from data stored within the system in some sort of file, from data input during the period in question, or to be the result of some processing. I then invite the students, individually or in pairs, to mark each of the data items with an **F, I** or **P**. Next, I draw up a table headed **F, I, P** and write their results in the appropriate column.

File	Input	Processing
Account number Name and address Previous reading	Account number Date of account Present reading	Cubic feet Therms Charges ....

Figure 9.2   Systems design table

Once this has been done, with unobtrusive help if needed, I congratulate them on becoming systems designers; they have specified the files, inputs and programs required to produce a given piece of computer output. One important point is that the exercise starts from something familiar. It thereby obviates the need to hand out six pages of explanatory notes before people can make a start. It has the right degree of difficulty and takes the right amount of time. It is unusual in that it is an example of the sequence 'do, then teach' used with a hard topic. The reason for this is twofold:

- The example chosen is sufficiently easy for students to be able to attempt it without lengthy instructions being necessary.
- It is as much motivational as technical; the course objective is not the hard one of turning them into designers. If this were the case I would be concerned that they got the solution completely right. As it is I am teaching hard/soft, aiming merely to convince them that they are capable of contributing to the development of systems that they will subsequently use.

Formatting a spreadsheet
The gas bill is an example of a simple, short exercise done in plenary session. Reinforcement and practice exercises usually take longer and

require splitting people into groups. When such groups require help, as with a 'hands-on' exercise, there is a finite number that can be run at any one time. If we find ourselves with six pairs of people, new to micros, all trying to master spreadsheets, databases or desktop publishing simultaneously we will run into problems. At any one time, at least two groups are likely to need assistance to get them out of a mess. Motivation will drop if we cannot quickly help them make progress.

The latter is a not untypical scenario. The question is: 'What do we do about it?' The first rule is: Never confuse the occurrence of a problem with the cause of a problem. It has happened in the middle of a session. If unsolved it will cause students to criticize the course presentation, and by implication, the lecturer. But the cause of the problem is a faulty specification. Twelve people trying to attain mastery of a complex technique or piece of software is too many for one lecturer to handle. Twelve people can be given a demonstration; 'hands-on' is a different matter. This analysis of the problem is of little help to the instructor at the time. The *presentation* solution would have been to grab a helper for just this session; the *specification* solution is to rewrite the objectives, reduce the number of students, or specify that two instructors are needed. The *writing* solution is to rewrite the exercise so as to make it capable of being run by one person. This means making it foolproof — never easy, given the extreme ingenuity of fools.

You enter:	You should see:	Comment:
1. SC#	Supercalc Header	
2. Any key	Blank spreadsheet	Column width = 9
3. "London#	'London' in A1	Cursor moves to B1
4. "Milan#	'Milan' in B1	Cursor moves to C1
5. "Brussels#	'Brussels' in C1	Cursor moves to D1
6. "Total#	'Total in D1'	Cursor moves to D1
7. Move cursor to D2 using direction keys		
8. SUM (A2:C2) #	'0' in D2	
9. Reposition cursor over D2	Form = (A2 : C2)	
10. /	Enter B,C,D . . . Z?	Command codes
11. R	From? (enter range), .	Asking for range
12. D2 #	To? (enter range), . . .	off copied cells
13. D3 : D6 #	Zeroes on column D	
14. Move cursor to A2		
15. 127.62 #	126.62 in A2 and D2	

Figure 9.3   Example of a spreadsheet exercise

The exercise, shown in Figure 9.3, running to 26 instructions in all, was written to get round the 'hands-on' problem. It details exactly which key the student has to press, what he will see on the screen as a result, and a brief explanation of what is happening. The result? Confidence-building for the students, reduced stress for the instructor.

Let us examine a typical course exercise to show an example of a presenter's guide and student's briefing notes. The following example is taken from the 'Training the Trainers' course. The presenter's guide first explains the options open to the presenter and then advises how to decide which exercises to use and how to run them. The student's briefing note gives them instructions on how to complete the exercise, together with information they will require to work the session.

'Training the Trainers' — Writing and Presentation of a Training Session

Presenter's guide

This is the major course exercise. Delegates are given approximately six hours in which to research and prepare a simulated training session. The session itself should last 45 minutes. You should tell groups to prepare a 30-minute presentation in order to allow time for questions.

Timetabling

The groups' presentations will be the last session of the course immediately following lunch on day 4. You should arrange a cold buffet lunch so that groups can reduce eating time to a minimum (they are certain to be behind schedule). Following the presentations you will make comments on their content and style and then conclude the course.

The morning of day 4 should be left free for preparation. A further two hours' preparation time should be found on day 3. This is at the discretion of the course director although the period immediately after lunch is advised.

Selection of exercises

Six exercises are available, all calling for a mixture of lecturing and demonstrations. The latter can be extended to include 'hands-on' by a person from a different group. The topics for the exercise are:

- Computer-based training (CBT)
- Desktop publishing (DTP)

- Spreadsheets
- Personal databases
- The use of films and filming to the trainer
- Telephone techniques

It is recommended that the first two are standard on any course. This is because CBT is of intrinsic interest to all trainers and DTP is an excellent topic and a technique that is directly relevant to trainers in the preparation of course manuals and visuals. Selection of the remaining one (or two) exercises is dependent on the interests and experience of the delegates. All groups should do different exercises.

Composition of groups

The exercises are written to be done in groups of three people. Where course numbers necessitate groups of four, the best exercises for this are CBT and Filming (see briefing notes).

The delegate profile filled in by students prior to the course asks them to indicate topics in which they are interested. This can be used as a guide to assigning people to groups. Alternatively, the course director can give the choice to the students. Knowledge of the topic is not a bar to being assigned that topic to present. However, delegates should *not* be assigned a topic which they have experience of teaching. Beyond this the following guidelines have been found useful:

- Delegates with a financial background will take readily to spreadsheets.
- Delegates with a background in sales or marketing will enjoy desktop publishing or telephone techniques.
- Delegates from personnel departments can be given the database exercise with a suggestion that they construct a personal database.
- Experienced trainers should be assigned to CBT.

Equipment required

The first four topics require a personal computer. Ideally there should be one computer for each group. The appropriate software is also required, as are operating manuals for all topics. Art books (refer course equipment list) should be available to assist in creating visuals. Access to a photocopier able to make overhead projector slides is invaluable.

Skills required

For those topics that use a personal computer the group requires someone with keyboard skills (particularly for desktop publishing). Computer literacy is *not* essential. All software used is 'user-friendly' and part of the exercise consists in showing how accessible the techniques are. If the class includes anyone with computer programming skills he is best assigned to the exercise on computer-based training as this includes the use of an authoring language for which programming experience is helpful but not obligatory.

Sequence of presentations
There is no prescribed order for presentations and course directors are recommended to make their own decision based on their assessment of the quality of the presentations. Essentially this means putting the best presentation last in order to finish on a high note. (This sequencing should not be divulged to delegates!)

Student's Briefing Note

Desk-Top Publishing (DTP)
This is the final course exercise. It is your opportunity, in syndicate, to write and present a complete session. Use it to put into practice all that you have learned on the course. You have approximately six hours in which to prepare your presentation. This should give you sufficient time to master the subject matter and put together a professional presentation. The presentation should last around 45 minutes. It will be filmed so that you can review it after the course.

The subject matter has been chosen to combine 'chalk and talk' with 'hands-on'. You should decide the division of the presentation between yourselves, though a generalized structure is given below. Try to ensure that all members of your group have an equal share in the presentation and have the opportunity to practise in the area that they will find most useful to them rather than that in which they have most experience.

General structure
The subject of your lecture lends itself to a mixture of education and training. The educative part is the general explanation of what DTP is. It should concentrate on those features that are common to all DTP, both how it works and what it is used for. You must assume that people in the audience will subsequently use a diversity of DTP software in their respective companies so that what you say must be applicable across the board.

The final part of the session will be a demonstration of a specific DTP package. Your session should include selecting an individual to do simple operations, such as changing typeface and print size, justifying text and adding an illustration. If you have the time, you can write a simple exercise for the person to undertake.

The bridge between the general introduction and the 'hands-on' session could be an explanation, using the OHP, of what the students will see during the 'hands-on' session. This gives them the chance to ask questions while there is still plenty of room to see what is going on (things get cramped during the 'hands-on').

The next page of this handout gives you some general information about DTP. You may assume that this session is on day 2 of an introductory course on 'Making Computers Work for You'. The students are a mixed bag of managers who are evaluating new techniques. For anyone likely to use DTP extensively in their own work, a follow-up two-day course is available. Your teaching objective is not therefore to make them experts in DTP but to enable them to understand what it is and how it could help them.

Some initial information about DTP

1. DTP allows people to do their own typesetting. To use the software, only keyboard skills and some initial training is required. The enclosed example of a marketing newsletter was completely typeset in-house. Only graphic design is required in order to present camera-ready artwork to the printer.

2. The most significant benefit is not the saving in cost (although this can be considerable) but the convenience. Copy can be easily changed without the delay of sending it back to the printer. Limited runs of highly volatile documents — such as course leaflets, where new dates have continually to be shown — give great flexibility.

3. Because manuals and promotional material is produced in-house, it is easy to prepare different versions for different markets. The enclosed newsletter is printed with different versions for the Benelux, Middle East and Australian markets.

4. You may take £2500 as the basic entry price for the computer hardware and software and an additional £2500 for a laser printer. Prices of the latter are falling. The market leader is the Apple Mac (which you have) but all self-respecting microcomputers now have some form of DTP software.

5. All DTP software will have the following facilities: multiple typefaces (called 'fonts') and sizes, justification, cut and paste, graphics tools, etc . . .

Additional information about DTP is contained in the attached articles.

In addition to these notes, delegates are given suppliers' brochures, an operating manual and articles about desktop publishing culled from the trade press. These amount to about a dozen pages for them to read and assimilate. This is so that the exercise includes research into the topic. The other point to notice about the briefing note is that it gives the instructor some free time while delegates are constructing their session from the information given. This is important as there may be four separate groups writing sessions on different topics each of which involves mastering some equipment or software. By providing extensive background information the writer releases the instructor to help the group member designated to do the 'hands-on' part of the session to learn the equipment. The amount of information contained in the briefing note also helps to make the course more easily learned by a new instructor and of a more consistent quality.

10
Writing soft

When writing hard courses the material is essentially fixed. The course writer has no personal standpoint regarding the material, only about how best to communicate it. With soft topics, the course writer's own opinions become relevant. As we have seen, soft courses deal more in persuasion and less in proof and the first essential is that the writer is himself persuaded of the validity of what is being taught. Soft courses tread a tightrope between being too specific and having one's treatment of the material challenged by the students, and being insufficiently specific and opting out of giving a lead.

Writing lectures

To see how we develop material, and how we harden it up without being accused of 'painting by numbers', let us take a specific example, that of a session on interviewing. We may remind ourselves first that the survey in Chapter 1 gave interviewing an average mark of only 3.3 for hardness. The general perception is that interviewing is something that some people are naturally better at than others. Our teaching task is to correct this impression by showing that effective interviewing can be learned. We can achieve this through a five-step process:

1. Define the topic
2. Identify the techniques
3. Structure the material
4. Write the material
5. Enhance the material.

Define the topic
Specify the exact problem in terms of setting boundaries. The wider we draw the boundary, the more difficult it will be to harden the topic as the more environments we shall have to take into account, the more exceptions there will be to any rules. There are many different types of interviews — data gathering, recruitment, disciplinary — in many

different environments — business, school, medical and so on. Does our material have to cover all these or can we restrict it to only some? Widening the net will make our task more difficult. There is a rough division between interviews which are mainly eliciting information — systems investigation, medical examinations — and those where the interviewer already possesses most of the information — disciplinary, recruitment. Devising hard rules to cover such a divergence will be difficult.

Identify the techniques

Investigate how the particular task is carried out. We need to identify an exhaustive list of all ways of carrying out the particular activity and describe each of them. We can identify two basic ways in which we carry out this step. The most obvious, and simplest (because the hardening up is done for you) is to read books on the subject. The second is to do the research for oneself. Typically this is done by studying a cross-section of people who do the activity well (though we should never ignore mistakes — the latter are always more fun, and often more instructive, than doing everything right).

What techniques do people — in particular those people who are good at interviewing — use? One type of interview not listed above is the 'talk show'. People who conduct these tend to earn very large sums of money. We may take this as a rough indication that they know what they are doing. Yet if we study them they appear to do nothing special. Just ask a few questions and let the interviewee do the talking. Not a bad way of earning £100 000 or more a year! But perhaps we have already hit on something — one of the rules:

- The interviewee should do most of the talking.

There is something else that is noticeable. The interview very rarely dries up. Nor does the interviewer ask anything to which the interviewee does not appear to have a good, sometimes amusing, answer. Maybe some preparation has gone into thinking up the questions; possibly even some background research. We have the makings of another rule — indeed one which is probably the hardest we will come across:

- The secret of interviewing lies in preparation.

If we extend our study into the area of political interviewing we quickly realize the importance of this rule. Politicians are so adept at not answering questions that the interviewer has to have prepared two or three levels of questions to have any hope of pinning the interviewee down. The interviewer has to look for any conflict between the answer given and party policy or answers given at other times. This gives us a third rule:

- Be a good listener.

By pursuing this approach we can devise a series of rules and guidelines for effective interviewing both at the general level of those quoted and at the detailed level of 'Always have a spare pen in case your normal one dries up'.

Structure the material

Organize the teaching points into a hierarchy. As illustrated by the example, the investigation throws up ideas in random order and at different levels of abstraction. We need to impose a structure on these. Some of the techniques may be hard and therefore of general application; these we write down as rules. Others may be environment- or person-dependent; these we write as guidelines with material on where and when to use them, and how to adapt them to a particular environment. (If we want to blur the distinction between these two different classes we can write them up under a heading 'dos and don'ts', leaving the student to form his own view on the status of each of the recommendations.)

The commonalities we discover between different types of interviews give us our basic structure:

- Preparation
- Conduct of interview
- Follow-up.

These are the basic processes. We then break these down into procedures. 'Conduct of interview' may break down into:

- Introduction
- Prepared questions
- Supplementary questions
- Note-taking
- Conclusion.

Questions may be further analysed into:

- Closed questions
- Open questions
- Alternative questions
- Suggestive questions
- Leading questions
- Check questions

We have developed a standard structure for an interview and broken this into procedures. At the procedural level we have identified rules and guidelines: 'Always explain the purpose of the interview', 'Maintain eye contact', 'Write up your summary as soon as possible after the interview'. In addition we have given students an analysis of types of questions and guidance on when to use which type.

Write the material

The above 'rules' are the basis of the lectures and student manual. We also need to give students practice in applying what they have been taught. Since interviewing is an interpersonal skill this needs to be through some form of role-playing. We therefore write an interview exercise and see how well the student applies the techniques he has been taught. The role-play will be constructed in such a way as to reinforce the main techniques.

Enhance the material

Many books have been written on interviewing techniques. However, we are teaching interviewing in a specific environment. In my case I teach interviewing in the context of a systems investigation. Despite the millions of words written about interviewing (or because we have not located the right ones), we may still run across problems specific to our own environment. There are two problems which if not unique to systems investigation, are at least of greater significance in this environment. They stem from the fact that the likely end-product of the investigation will be a computer system. Computers like to have things cut and dried (an expression synonymous with 'hard'). Therefore the interviewer has to do two things:

- Tease out the exception conditions — things that only happen occasionally under special sets of circumstances. Failure to identify these will result in an inadequate specification of the new system.
- Tie people down to specific answers. If he asks the question: 'What is the budget for developing the new system?', he must not be satisfied with a vague answer — 'I haven't really devoted any thought to that. Perhaps you can come up with a figure . . .'.

My hardening up of this subset of interviewing skills stems directly from my experience of role-playing interviewees. At the end of each interview I need to make constructive criticism about how well it was carried out. When interviewers manifestly fail to elicit important information you have to explain to them why this is the case. Over a period of time, one notices that some interviewers gather more information than others. The next question is: 'What are these people doing differently from those who are less successful?' If we can determine that, we can tell the other people what they should be doing — we can write new tips. We profit from the greater experience or ability of the successful to impart the techniques to others.

One of the main observed differences between those who obtain a clear answer about the project deadline and those who allow themselves to be fobbed off with a vague one, is that the former are more persistent than the latter. We therefore update our lecture notes by pointing out the virtues of persistence. However 'Be persistent' like 'Be prepared' is a bit soft. Persistence does not entail grabbing the interviewee by the throat and choking an answer out of him; it takes the form of asking the question in a different way.

"Look, I'll ask you just one more time......"

An effective technique for dealing with people who profess to have no idea about a deadline or budget is to pick a date or figure at random:

'What development cost do you envisage for the new system?'
'I really have no yardstick by which to measure it.'
'But we are talking in terms of a quarter of a million pounds?'
'Oh, nothing like that.'
'Fifty thousand . . .?'
'I would expect to spend more than that on a project of this type.'
'Two hundred thousand?'
'Somewhere in that region.'

And so on. This is another example of the rule which we have come across in teaching but which holds equally true for interviewing:

● Be specific.

It is by this process of feedback from classroom to writing that lectures and courses improve with age. Nevertheless, we have all run across courses which have remained unchanged over decades. This observation allows me to end this section with a 'meta-rule', not about interviewing but about course development:

- Courses improve when teachers view them as a learning opportunity for themselves as well as for students.

Writing soft exercises

As we have seen it will be ineffective to teach interviewing without some form of practical work to enable students to apply what they have been taught. Because our research has resulted in a specific set of techniques we should in this instance put the practical work after the lecture. On other occasions we may reverse this sequence. The following examples give excellent insights into how soft topics can be tackled in such a way as to allow participants to think for themselves and then be guided towards generalizing the experience gained through the exercise, so that later they will be able to apply it to their own work or personal situation.

Example 1: ranking — an exercise in decision-making

How do we teach people to make good decisions? Is the process purely intuitive and therefore non-teachable, reducible to a set of rules or somewhere in-between?

The following exercise is taken from a course on technical leadership written by Jerry Weinberg and Daniel Freedman. It is a model for all that this book puts forward in teaching a soft subject. I shall describe the exercise and then relate it back to our guidelines for hardening up.

Students are given a list with 15 entries such as those shown below and asked to rank them in order by length (or height):

- The world's tallest hedge
- The diameter of the largest pancake
- The widest moustache (when fully extended)
- The longest worm
- The tallest man
- The diameter of the largest omelette.

After each student has individually ranked the entries they are grouped into four teams and instructed to produce a team ranking. Each of the teams is given a different briefing note on how to come to this decision. The four briefing notes given are for voting, decision by the team leader, consensus and fighting for one's own decision.

1. *Voting* Under this system the team arrives at a collective decision about the ranking by taking the average of each team member's own

rankings. No discussion is necessary and the process is therefore quick.

2. *The leader decides* A team leader is appointed. The team ranking becomes his responsibility. He can confer and discuss rankings with his team members and be guided by them to whatever extent he thinks will optimize the final decision. But the final decision is his. The latter rule means that this is usually the second fastest of the four groups to come to a decision.

3. *Consensus* This group does not have a leader. Ranking is done by consensus and the final decision is one to which all members are willing to subscribe. Obviously this means that individuals, for the sake of coming to a collective decision, concur in some markings about which they have reservations. This process is longer than the two previous because of the lack of one person with the authority to cut short discussion.

....Everyone fights for their own opinion.

4. *Fight it out* Individuals are instructed that their aim is to make the group ranking as close as possible to their own. In other words everyone fights for their own opinion. Clearly this strategy makes a collective decision logically impossible and after a while the group informally abandons it in favour of one of the other three. But not before they have discovered something about the difficulty of decision-making when people refuse to compromise!

When all teams have decided their rankings, the right answer is given. Notice again that the exercise has a hard solution so that which team did best is not itself a matter of opinion. The correct ranking is compared with individual's own solutions and with that of the teams. Some fancy

111

mathematics enables a 'percentage correct' figure to be calculated for all solutions.

The fun and learning starts with the many comparisons that can be made:

- Which decision-making strategy produced the best absolute ranking?
- Which strategy showed the greatest or least improvement over the average of its individuals' own rankings?
- How did individual rankings compare with team rankings?
- Did any individual in the 'consensus' team concur in a ranking that was inferior to his own (the 'wimp' test)?

Note that this is an *educational* exercise. Our earlier analysis of this type of teaching said that it requires experienced lecturers able to think on their feet. This is eminently the case with this exercise because the teacher has no way of knowing in advance what the results will be of the above comparisons. He cannot have a handout at the ready extolling the superiority of the consultative strategy if this team's ranking comes last and is inferior to the average of its members. He is aware of the pros and cons of the different decision-making strategies and of what is therefore statistically the most likely outcome, but cannot guarantee that any particular occurrence will conform to this.

Decision-making is environment-dependent in that the strategy is influenced by the type of decision that is at stake. A decision as to which pub to go to for lunch is one where speed is of the essence and the actual decision of minor importance. It is thus probably best made by informal voting; a decision to abort a million pound project may require a little longer. We cannot therefore definitively proclaim that one strategy is superior to another. Hardening up consists of analysing the circumstances which influence the choice of strategy.

Decision-making is also person-dependent in that some people are naturally more prone to discussion where others prefer to back their own judgement. It is very difficult to persuade someone of the merits of broadening or changing their own preferred style merely by lecturing at them on alternative strategies. By using an exercise such as that described, people can see for themselves the merits of different styles. We do not teach; we help to learn.

There are several frameworks for exercises which enable the writer to construct an exercise relevant to his own environment. Typical of these are action maze and in-basket exercises.

Example 2: action maze

Here students, individually or in teams, are confronted with a problem on which they have to make a decision. A typical one could be that of a subordinate who has recently started arriving late for work. A menu of choices is presented from which one must be chosen. Depending on which is chosen the team is given more information and asked to make a further decision. Thus a first decision to find out more before confronting the person might produce information which helps to explain the conduct (e.g. a family crisis), whereas a decision to discipline the person might lead to a resignation. The 'maze' element is in the many different paths that the course writer charts through the exercise depending on the decisions the teams make. The writer can design responses and paths to illustrate the teaching points he wishes to make. Teams may complete the exercise before class discussion or there can be a discussion after each round.

Example 3: in-basket

In this exercise the course writer constructs the contents of a typical manager's in-tray. A dozen or so items, ranging from the important to the trivial, the urgent to the timeless, the political to the social, are handed to students. They are instructed to sort them into priority and to indicate how they would deal with them. A typical list might include:

- A letter of resignation from a subordinate
- A memo from the managing director calling for submission of budgets
- Junk mail
- A reminder to write a presentation for a meeting next week

- A visa application for an imminent overseas trip
- An expense claim form.

The course writer constructs the in-basket in such a way as to bring out whatever points about prioritizing, delegation and so on that he wishes to make. Simulations constructed using the above skeletons are flexible, easy to write and easy to enhance. Note, characteristically, that both action mazes and in-baskets work on a 'do, then teach' sequence.

I have earlier emphasized the importance of enhancing exercises based on experience gained when running them. Any fool can lift an exercise from a book and include it unamended in a course. The skilful writer packages the exercise and in so doing improves it. The following exercise is widely used on communication courses. Here we see how the writer has taken the exercise, extended the number of teaching points and written a comprehensive guide to ensure that maximum benefit is gained from it.

Example 4: six tables

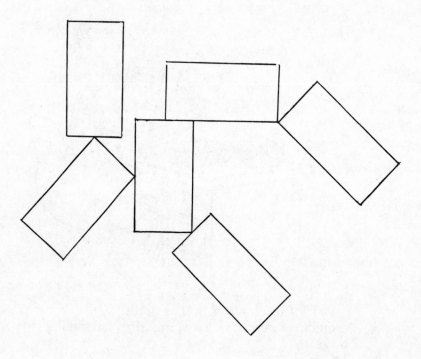

One student is given a set of shapes (referred to as 'tables' to give artistic verisimilitude to an otherwise bald and unconvincing narrative), and asked to describe it for the rest of the class to reproduce. The description is done initially as a one-way exercise with the victim placed behind some barrier designed to inhibit feedback. The exercise is then repeated with a different set of shapes. This time the audience is allowed to ask questions in order to clarify the description. At the end the results of the two descriptions are compared.

The main teaching point of the exercise is to demonstrate the superiority of two-way communication over one-way. (Actually I prefer to say it is the 'difference' between the two. The simplest way to communicate the pattern would be to photocopy it!) But there are many more teaching points to be made than just the supposed superiority of two-way communication. The writer needs to draw as many teaching points from the exercise as possible and show how the ability to reproduce a set of tables relates to the field of communication generally. He therefore writes a students' handout in the form of an analysis.

Students' handout
Teaching points contained in this exercise:

1. *Preparation* Most people rush into explaining the shape without adequate preparation. This is almost inevitable given that it is sprung on them and the rest of the class is waiting with pencils poised. However, it is worth considering how much better one would complete the exercise if given an hour to prepare.
2. *Pictures speak louder than words* A very obvious point in this exercise. However, we are frequently called upon to describe in words something for which the more appropriate medium is pictures. Giving directions over the telephone on how to get somewhere is one example; a telex message instead of fax is another. We cannot always choose our medium.
3. *Feedback* The most basic lesson is the importance of feedback in any communication. Two-way communication is more time-consuming than one-way — consultation is a lengthy process. Its justification is the superiority of the end result.
4. *Sequence* A common mistake — caused by our 'mind-set' — is to start at one of the corners, proceeding downwards and left to right. In fact, it is much better to start from the middle and work out; this reduces the dependency of one table on another and therefore lessens the impact of a mistake by the receiver.
5. *Richness of conceptual language* The more concepts we can utilize in a given communication, the greater our chances of success.

In this exercise there is a number of different (and therefore reinforcing) concepts that can be used:

- Geometry
- Compass points
- Graphic design (landscape/portrait)
- Alphabetic (T-shaped)
- Analogies ('like a herring-bone').

Saying something in two different ways is the classic means of verifying the accuracy of the receipt of a message.

6. *Analysis* If one analyses the exercise it becomes apparent that the recipient needs to get two things right — the direction of the table, and its alignment with (or relationship to) the other tables. By splitting our description of each table into these two separate components, we can explain the layout much more accurately and easily.

7. *Definitions* Communication is fundamentally the meaning of words. Words are often ambiguous. What does 'touching' mean in the context of this exercise? Touching at one point only, or running alongside? It helps to bring out this difference and define separate terms for these two meanings before starting on the explanation.

   Similarly, it is of great assistance if some other ground rules are made clear — for example, all tables are the same shape and size; their dimensions are length equals twice width.

8. *We learn by experience — or do we?* Confronted with the same exercise again people show a tremendous improvement — but only if they have consciously taken the effort to learn from the first one!

The analysis ensures that no teaching point contained in the exercise gets omitted. It guarantees consistency of approach between different lecturers running the same course. But the course writer still needs to ensure that the exercise is properly run. To do this he writes a presenter's guide:

Presenter's guide

Purpose of exercise
This exercise serves to initiate a session on styles of communication. Specifically it demonstrates the difference between one-way and two-way communication (and between pictures and words). Other

two-way communication (and between pictures and words). Other teaching points are as documented in the relevant student handout. The exercise consists of getting a student to describe verbally a diagram (described as being of six tables) for the remainder of the class to reproduce. This is done twice, using a different diagram for the second go. The first time the class are not allowed to ask any questions; the second time they may. One point of the exercise is to demonstrate the superiority of two-way communication over one-way. It helps, therefore, if students' second attempts show an improvement on their first!

Running the Exercise
1. Select a student to give the description. Bearing in mind that we want the first attempt to be relatively unsuccessful you should be careful in your choice. Steer clear of keen sailors or anyone with a known interest or work that may make them good at describing the diagram.
2. Explain the exercise to the class:

   'You are to set up a lecture room containing six tables for a colleague. He promised to ring you during the day to describe how he wanted them laid out — which is in a slightly odd arrangement. Unfortunately, he was unable to contact you and had to leave instructions on the company's answering machine. It is this description which you will now hear. The tape self-destructs at the end. Your job is to draw the layout of the tables.'

3. Give the diagram of the layout of the tables to the selected student and place him behind a screen to inhibit non-verbal communication. Tell him to start when he is ready. Make a note of how long he waits before starting (see 'preparation' in the student handout).
4. Time both descriptions. This is to enable you to make the point that two-way communication is more time-consuming than one-way. On average the first description will take around four minutes and the second around ten.
5. During this, and the second, description make a note of the communication problems that arise and how they are overcome.
6. At the end of the first description show delegates the diagram and ask them to count how many tables were in the correct position. Log this score.
7. Give the second version of the table layout to the student. Explain that this time the class may ask questions in order to clarify anything they do not understand.

> 8. At the end of the second description show delegates the diagram and compare the accuracy of this attempt with that of the first. Usually all delegates should have the second diagram completely correct.
> 9. Ask delegates to explain the improvement and lead the discussion towards the points in the handout.

Finally, let us look at the integration of exercise and lecture in teaching people to write more clearly.

Example 5: fog index

The fog index is an excellent example of how people attempt to harden up a soft subject. Writing is an art; arts are soft. Yet almost everyone needs to learn to write clearly in their work. The fog index attempts to make writing more easily teachable by taking the subjectivity out of style. It states that the clearness of a piece of writing is a function of the average sentence length and the percentage of long words (defined as words of three syllables or more). Multiplying these together (and multiplying by 0.4), gives you the fog index of any piece of writing.*

As a teaching exercise it is an interesting contrast to the 'six tables'. The former has a specific solution which students try to reach through using a soft (i.e. non-formalized) approach; teaching consists of showing that it is possible to devise a set of guidelines to help in the process. The fog index has hard rules (a mathematical calculation) leading to agreement on the value of the index of a given piece of prose. The extent to which this removes subjectivity from writing is a typical soft/hard argument.

Presenter's guide

Purpose of exercise
To show that you write more clearly by using shorter sentences and shorter words. The exercise consists of examining a sample piece of prose and then rewriting it in a simpler form. The latter task can be done individually or by the class as a whole. In the latter case, the exercise should take approximately 30 minutes; if undertaken individually it will require an additional 15 minutes.

---

*The multiplication by 0.4 is a classic example of hardening up a soft subject. The number thus obtained (say $30 \times 0.4 = 12$) purports to show the number of years' schooling necessary to read the piece of writing in question. Thus a fog index of 12 indicates that a person would need to have been at school for 12 years to be able to understand something written at this level.

1. Hand out article from *The Australian*. Explain that the article was culled from the editorial page. Either *The Australian*'s leader writers have a mission to confuse or we caught them on a bad day.
2. Ask delegates individually to calculate the fog index. The answer is:

   Sentence length 217/7 = 31
   Long words: 217/39 (excluding proper nouns) = 18%
   Fog index (31+18) × 0.4 = 19

3. Explain, with examples, how we reduce the 'fog' in our writing:

   - Split long sentences into two
   - Substitute short words, such as, 'try', for long words, such as 'endeavour'
   - Cross out superfluous words and expressions
   - Replace long-winded phrases 'at this point in time' by shorter — 'now'.

4. Individually, or collectively, rewrite all or part of the article.
5. Hand out the revised version. Discuss the rewritten article. Is it a good rewrite? What improvements could be made? How soft is good writing? Do delegates find the fox index useful? Should we at all times try to write more simply?

Handout 4.1: original version

Deep concern over unrest in Sabah

The turmoil and violence disrupting the Malaysian State of Sabah have their immediate causes in a complex dispute between the local political parties. But to a substantial extent the origin of the divisions within this small society which have caused the present bitterness can be found in the rise of militant Islamic fundamentalism.

One of the most ominous aspects of the rioting that has occurred for over a week is the active role being played by Muslim immigrants from the Philippines. The immigrants' participation in the Sabah disturbances is unlikely to be the result of their having become absorbed in the intricacies of the State's politics, but is further evidence that the new wave of Islamic militancy has no regard for national frontiers.

Islamic fundamentalism has already created a ruthless, totalitarian regime in Iran and has helped to tear Lebanon apart. It was responsible for the murder of Egypt's President Sadat and poses a constant threat to the more moderate Arab governments and those many millions of Muslims who are neither fanatical nor irrational.

So far the countries in South-East Asia with large Muslim populations have remained relatively unscathed, although the strength of resurgent Islam is evident in Pakistan, Bangladesh and Indonesia, and has had an obvious influence on government policies in each of those nations.

The Australian, 21 March 1986

Handout 4.2: revised version (figures in parentheses are sentence length and number of long words)

Deep concern over unrest in Sabah

The violence in the Malaysian State of Sabah has its immediate cause in a complex dispute between the local political parties. (21,3) But the divisions within this small society which have caused the present bitterness originate largely in the rise of militant Islamic fundamentalism. (22,6)

The rioting has been going on for over a week. (10,0) One of its most ominous aspects is the active role being played by Muslim immigrants from the Philippines. (18,2) Their involvement is nothing to do with local politics. (9,2) It is further evidence that the new wave of Islamic militancy has no regard for national frontiers. (17,3)

Islamic fundamentalism has already created a ruthless, totalitarian regime in Iran. (11,3) It has helped to tear Lebanon apart. (7,0) It was responsible for the murder of Egypt's President Sadat. (10,1) It poses a constant threat to the more moderate Arab governments and to those many millions of Muslims who are neither fanatical nor irrational. (24,4)

So far the countries in South-East Asia with large Muslim populations have remained relatively unscathed. (15,2) However, the strength of resurgent Islam is evident in Pakistan, Bangladesh and Indonesia and has had an obvious influence on government policies in each of those nations. (27,7)

Sentence length: 191/12 = 16
Long words: 33/191 = 16
Fog index 12.8

There is no reason why the presenter's guide should not include suggestions for humour, anecdotes and illustrative examples:

- An analysis using the fog index was done on communications from the directors to the workforce of the former British Leyland car manufacturers. Most of the communications had a fog index of over 18 making them effectively unintelligible. The only communication below the level of 14 was 'Happy New Year'.
- In an experiment in the United States, masters' theses were submitted for professorial marking in two separate forms — first, as written, secondly, after being simplified by reducing the 'fog'. Great care was taken not to change the sense in any way in simplifying them. All theses received higher marks in their 'before' rather than 'after' state!

How to get the most from exercises

Through an analysis of the examples of different types of exercises, including case studies which are covered in the next chapter, we can devise a set of guidelines for their creation and improvement.

- An exercise should contain a number of teaching points clearly related to the course objectives; the instructor should be aware of these and of how to use the exercise to bring them out.
- The writer must decide on how to integrate the exercise with the teaching — specifically, whether it should be run before or after the teaching session to which it is relevant.
- An exercise must be totally relevant to the topic in hand. It cannot be dragged in just as an easy way to break up a session.
- Clear briefing notes are an invaluable aid to successful practical work and in taking the strain off the course presenter.
- On short courses look for an example which cuts down the amount of background briefing required; on longer courses consider extending one basic exercise throughout the course to achieve the same end.
- The writer must decide whether an exercise should be run with students tackling it individually or together, in class or separate groups. As a guide, the shorter and simpler the exercise, the better it is done in class and individually; the longer and more complex, the better it is tackled in groups. Soft topics are conducive to group discussion; coaching demands an individual attempt.
- Exercises must be carefully graded so as to provide the right level of challenge. Exercises that are either too trivial or too difficult are demotivators. The right level may only be achieved after the exercise has been run a number of times.
- Frequently when an exercise is run, groups or individuals will finish

at different times. A difference of a few minutes is trivial; a delay of an hour whilst faster groups wait for slower ones to catch up can again mean a loss of motivation. The writer's solution is to make the exercise open-ended, allowing some syndicates to progress further than others, or to provide a supplementary exercise. The timetabling solution is for the exercise to precede a break so that a faster group can take an early coffee or disappear to the bar.

- If the course is to be run in different parts of the world, the exercise must travel well. Some years ago I developed a flowcharting exercise based on the calculation of a cricketer's batting average. It neatly showed the typical errors that you get in logic diagrams and the difficulty of finding them all and had good potential for humour. Unfortunately all this was lost on my audiences in non-cricketing parts of the world.

11

Case studies

A case study is an extended exercise involving a reasonably complex set of issues based on real life or a close representation thereof. The intention is to give students practice in a situation as close to life as can be devised within the confines of a course. It will usually entail splitting the course into groups. On most occasions all groups will work on the same case study, comparing results at the end; in some circumstances different aspects of a case study may be given to different groups and they subsequently bring their different views together.

A good case study is worth its weight in gold. It has a longer life than most teaching material for the simple reason that a case study poses problems whereas lectures teach solutions. Problems are universal and time-resistant; solutions are environment-, time- and people-dependent. In the computer industry, where technology and methods both change at a fast rate, the 'right' solution to a case study may change from year to year.

My systems analysis course has used the 'same' case study for the last 12 years, in all parts of the world. I put the word 'same' in inverted commas, because it is continually evolving; a case study is a system and systems require maintenance and enhancement. In the case study in question this has taken the form of increasing the size and complexity of the system as computers have become more powerful and 'user-friendly'.

Case studies are motivators. Frequently the presentation of solutions is the culmination of the course and involves much burning of midnight oil on the preceding night. However, as Drucker has pointed out, motivation is sustained through a series of short-term objectives, so it is important that the case study is structured in such a way that there are identifiable checkpoints, with clearly-specified deliverables, throughout the course. These serve the additional purpose of keeping the progress of syndicates reasonably uniform and of picking up any syndicate that is going off at a tangent. The case study mentioned above has four such checkpoints:

- Identification and agreement of user requirements

- Documentation of current system
- Problem analysis and transition to design
- Final presentation of syndicate's solutions.

The use of case studies

Case studies are appropriate to longer courses teaching techniques which are largely interdependent. A sales course will take students through the complete cycle from first client contact to close; a systems course will go from initial specification of the users' requirements through to the design of a new system. It is the interdependence more than any distinction between education, training and coaching, that influences our decision. As we have seen, dependency teaching requires feedback. For activities such as systems design or selling, this can only be achieved through a case study.

The presentation of solutions ... involves much burning of midnight oil

Even where a set of techniques is discrete we may still elect to utilize one case study throughout. The latter strategy may be used if we want to reduce the amount of background material that we hand out. Thus, in a five-day improving communications skills course, covering interviewing, report writing, meetings and presentations, it is sensible to use one case study. The output from one phase — interviewing — can then be used as the input to the next phase — report writing. In this instance, the techniques are not interdependent but they are linked by the case study for convenience. This, of course, does not preclude the use of other separate exercises.

Writing case studies

Developing a case study is a six-step process:

1. Identify the teaching points that it is being used to illustrate
2. Select the case example
3. Develop the script
4. Write briefing notes for the students
5. Write model solutions
6. Maintain and enhance the case study based on course experience.

Identify the teaching points

These will closely relate to the course objectives and teaching circle. On a high 'T' course the purpose of the case study will be to give practice in new methods, techniques or equipment. On 'C' courses they will be used to put students into a learning situation, such as a role-play, where they can develop their interpersonal skills. On 'E' courses they will be used as a means of forcing students to think for themselves or enabling them to apply environment-dependent teaching to a specific situation. The case study will work by setting problems related to the teaching points. Students will be required to identify and solve the problems using the methods and techniques taught in formal lectures.

Select the case example

Case studies can be acquired 'off-the-shelf' from commercial training companies, management schools or books. As with any package, it is unlikely to be precisely what you are looking for, but may involve a significant short-cut in the development process.

If one is writing one's own, an obvious source, given permission, is a project on which one has worked. Selecting a familiar company or project gives one in-depth knowledge and guarantees that all operating data will be realistic. There is also the confidence that goes with knowing that there is an actual answer to any question that a student might ask, even if you have to get on the telephone to find it out. The possibility of discrepancies in your facts — always present with a manufactured case study — is negligible. The danger is that the case study becomes one which only its writer can run. The writer must therefore take care to document all aspects. Building a complete script in this way will be materially assisted by rehearsal and quality reviews.

An alternative is to use a live system or project from the company for whom the course is being written. This has the advantage of combining teaching with consultancy and can result in significant progress or improvement being made on the project. It is most applicable when teaching hard subjects. Using in-company examples in teaching management skills may well be impolitic! However, even with hard subjects this approach has considerable drawbacks. The students will know more than the lecturer about the minutiae of the project or about their own environment and corporate culture. The real project is most unlikely to include all the features needed to draw out the points of a technique. It may simply be too big to handle. Case studies are always having to be pruned to fit within the available time.

If none of these alternatives is suitable or available you will need to invent your own. Even in this instance you will doubtless model your case on a familiar industry. Research then consists of gathering information about the industry and collating it into a case company with organization chart, number of employees, geographical location, product range and so on.

Develop the script

The script is information about the case company. It exists in two forms:

- That which is always given to the students
- That which is acquired by the students only if they ask the right questions.

This latter information may exist in the form of supplementary printed handouts — operating figures, additional documents, etc. — or it may be in the presenter's script and communicated verbally.

All scripts are unique to the company or project being described but their development commonly involves the following steps:

1. Describe the company/project. The students will require background information typically about the company's market, finance and products. The geographical siting of the company may be significant. Leading personalities may require character sketches.
2. Define the current situation and any problems or plans relevant to the exercise.
3. Create any background documents needed — balance sheet, procedure manual, product catalogue. Design any source documents that the students will need to examine.
4. Check the exercise for:

    - Consistency — I once discovered that the average delivery carried by a case company's vans was two packets of aspirins!
    - Credibility — systems should not be too ramshackle, buyers too eager, subordinates too awkward.
    - Timing — that it will run within the course timetable. If

this means excluding things which in real life would normally be within the study we need to make this explicit in our introduction.

Write briefing notes

The script gives information about the company. Briefing notes give information to the students about how they are to tackle the exercise. They will instruct, or give guidance, in the following:

- Who they (i.e. the group) are or represent. Frequently groups will be cast in the role of an outside consultancy, thereby explaining why it is they have no prior knowledge of the case company.
- Their immediate task — interview the chief accountant, contact a prospective buyer.
- Their next deliverable — an interview summary, sales proposal.
- How to go about the task (unless the teaching strategy is to throw them in at the deep end).
- Any ground rules — for example, whether they can ask the instructor for help.
- Timing — how long they have to undertake the task.

Write model solutions

The case study writer should always provide some guidance to the case study. In the case of a high 'T' course this will be the correct solution (including intermediate solutions if appropriate) at which groups are expected to arrive. For softer courses this will tend more towards an analysis of possible solutions with the pros and cons of each. Omission of any form of solution is a strong indication that the case study requires hardening up.

Maintain and enhance the case study

Case studies always embody some kind of system. Systems require maintenance and enhancement. Maintenance is fixing errors or bringing facts and figures up to date; enhancement is adding new problems, quirks, requirements aimed at making the case study more complicated. Both are usually necessary over a period of time, either because the teaching material changes and the case needs to reflect this, or because new technology changes the environment within which a solution is sought. The latter is a particular problem in courses on the design or use of computer systems. The cost/performance ratio, and accessibility of computers has changed so dramatically over the last 15 years that hitherto demanding problems overnight became trivial. If the course writer is also the presenter such problems are seen by him whilst running the course; if the course is being presented by others we need to arrange periodic reviews of the case study and use these to specify any required modifications.

A point that I have stressed about all communication is the importance of sequence. The sequence of this book is course specification, design, writing and presentation. How you run a case study is strictly part of the course presentation. However, we must never allow ourselves to become slaves of any one sequence. In books, as in courses, it may be sensible on occasions to depart from the overall sequence. This is my excuse for including the section on running case studies (which properly comes under presentation) in this section of the book. It is more logical to keep everything I have to say about case studies in the one chapter.

Running case studies

Good case studies, properly run, are an invaluable teaching aid. But they do not run themselves. Groups may get bogged down, they may find difficulty in coming to decisions, personality conflicts may arise. The presenter should therefore give careful thought to exactly how he is going to manage this part of the course. Running a case study comprises the following activities:

- Forming syndicates
- Running the syndicates
- Role-playing
- Evaluating presentations.

Forming syndicates
The first question is whether the case study is going to be worked on by the same syndicate for the duration of the course. If inter-syndicate transfers are not allowed, then particular care must be taken in choosing who will work with whom. The second question is 'Who decides?' Some trainers prefer to let the course form its own syndicates. This approach gains the benefit of greater identification with a self-devised, rather than externally-imposed solution. With in-company courses, the relevant manager may decide the syndicate assignments prior to the course. Whoever it is that makes the decision will do so on the basis of some predetermined criteria. The guidelines most commonly used in assigning syndicates are:

- Splitting up people from the same company
- Keeping people of similar status together (on an in-company course)
- Mixing different disciplines, such as programmers and users on a systems course, salesmen and customers on a negotiating course
- Putting language groups together where the audience is multi-national
- Having mixed or single-sex syndicates

- Putting all the smokers in one group
- Spreading different personality types around or keeping them in one group.

...... putting all the smokers in one group.

Some of these can be mutually-exclusive — all the smokers could be from the same company. Usually the trainer will have developed his own hierarchy through which he works, recognizing that this is a soft activity and that much will depend on the environment and the individuals.

Running the syndicates

This resolves itself into two separate issues — the rules within which syndicates work, and the amount of assistance that the trainer gives them. The first of these can be represented as a set of options between which the trainer can choose:

- Syndicates 'compete' with each other, working on the same case study.
- Syndicates co-operate with each other towards a common solution. This strategy is mostly employed when it is the only way of fitting the work into the available time. The case study is split into modules with syndicates developing their own part of the solution and then combining them. This may be a means of overcoming a time constraint which prevents all syndicates presenting separate solutions

How much assistance should the presenter give to syndicates? The skill here is in drawing the line between neglect and over-involvement, leaving them to get on by themselves as opposed to continually pulling up the tree to see whether it is still growing. The correct amount of help will partly be determined by the type of case study. On a high 'T' course the students will need plenty of instructor help to ensure that they are applying the techniques correctly. In a coaching situation there will be a high degree of instructor involvement in helping individual students develop their skills. In an 'E' environment the students may learn as much from syndicate discussions as they would from frequent advice or interference from the instructor. Equally, different groups on the same course may require different levels of assistance. The presenter must be flexible enough to recognize the signals and react accordingly.

The correct balance may vary through the course. At times, particularly early on, when participants are still finding their feet and have questions about the material that has been handed them, it is likely that the trainer will need to make frequent rounds of the syndicates. Nearing the end, as they prepare their presentations, the trainer is better off leaving them to their own devices.

There is another balance which we should be careful to preserve (the terminology of maintaining balance shows that running case studies is soft). We want a syndicate's solution to be one with which they are justly satisfied; but we do not want to do the job for them. Helping them at every turn may produce a better solution on the course but they will not have an instructor looking over their shoulder when they apply the techniques for real. On balance I believe the watchword should be 'benign neglect'.

Role-playing

Most case studies involve role-playing. An important decision is whether the instructor should always play one of the roles. Role-playing within a case study demands a close knowledge, not only of the case study script, but also of the teaching points to be brought out. If we are teaching soft we may use simulations where both sides of a role-play are undertaken by the delegates. We should realize that the problems of this are not twice that where only one 'variable' is involved — they are the square of the problems. The instructor cannot break into a role-play without destroying its credibility. Control of the simulation is therefore transferred to the participants, often with unpredictable results!

The reasons for this can be judged from the following guide to role-playing:

Know your script

The objective of most role-playing is that people should learn how to conduct interviews whether as part of an investigation, for counselling or for selling. In the first of these it is incumbent upon us to know all the answers since what we are teaching is how to get at the facts. It is hardly fair if the role-player does not himself know them! In the selling situation the role-player has to judge precisely how to react to any suggestion made by the salesman. The first instance I saw where a potential customer was role-played by a student the salesman was on a hiding to nothing. The student saw it as a challenge not to be sold anything; this was a competition in which he held all the cards. The second time the student role-player rolled on his back and asked to be shown where to sign the contract the minute the salesman uttered the magic word 'benefit'.

Never exit from the role
It destroys the integrity of the role-playing simulation if the role player suddenly reverts to being the instructor. This means that if we ever are caught out then we have to bluff our way through. In extremis use 'I'll get back to you later with that . . .'. External interruptions should be handled in role-playing mode if at all possible.

Don't say anything you can't believe
Perhaps my Thespian talents are inferior to those of other role-players but when I am lacking in confidence with my lines I suspect that this communicates itself to the students. It is therefore important that the basic case study be credible and that characters within it act credibly.

Decide what personality the interviewee is going to adopt
It is more interesting and more constructive if interviewees have different personalities. Students enjoy having different personalities to interview and indeed welcome a level of 'hamming'. Each interviewee should therefore be assigned a personality — enthusiastic or apathetic, helpful or hostile — as part of the script. Within this it is for the role-player to decide dynamically how to react. I adapt the role-playing to suit the interviewer. This means making the interviewee more helpful for a less experienced and nervous interviewer and more awkward with somebody with more experience. I also react to the interviewer's style — those that lead with their chin get it punched.

As always the role player must know what teaching points he is using the character to make. One of the teaching points about data gathering interviews is the necessity to pick up exceptions. In this case the role-player must drop hints in the interviews and see whether the student notices them and acts on them. With an inexperienced interviewer I will make it easier by using expressions such as 'normally' and 'generally speaking', with somebody that is a bit smarter I make it a bit more difficult by using intonation or throw-away comments such as 'it depends' and see whether they are followed up.

Play fair
Role-playing exercises are simulations. However well both sides act out the situation there is always an element of the contrived. Interviewees

131

know that they are 'on trial' and tend to act slightly differently from how they might in real life. In particular this is true with social 'chit-chat'. One role-player of my acquaintance used to trap people into explaining binary arithmetic and then criticize them for failure to keep the interview to the point. In real life, as we all know, time spent talking about irrelevancies, but which establish personal contact, is extremely valuable. In many parts of the world inattention to this would be considered impolite.

Decide on the role of the non-participating students
There is a number of possibilities for dealing with the other syndicate members. The 'fish bowl' approach leaves them as non-participating observers of the interview. This can lead to loss of motivation if the interview is a lengthy one. However, allowing them to take notes takes the pressure off the actual interviewer since he knows that he has a back-up if he fails to make proper notes himself. To get round this problem I tell the other students that they are not allowed to take notes about the information that is being communicated; however, they can do two other things. One is they can jot down any question they think that the interviewer misses; this is quite useful if he misses an obvious supple-mentary. It is more effective if the interviewer is told that by his colleagues than by the lecturer. Secondly, I ask them to think about the conduct of the interview and make any comments as to how it went. The combination of these gives them something to do whilst stopping them taking over the notetaking role of the interviewer.

Feedback on the interview
You cannot separate this from what you have said about interviewing in the lecture sessions. The feedback essentially is a commentary on how well the student has implemented the points you have made. Thus if you have emphasized following-up exceptions you comment on their use of supplementaries; if you have pointed out the importance of sequenc-ing the interview you look to see whether they followed a logical sequence or danced around all over the place; if you talked about how you control an interview (slowing down a fast talker or prompting a taciturn interviewee) then you comment on that.

Evaluating presentations
Presentations are frequently the climax of the course. The system of checkpoints should have ensured that no syndicate will present a really ill-thought-out solution. Allowing people to make mistakes is often an effective form of teaching. But they need to have made them in time for us to have corrected them, not as the last thing they do. This will only end the course on a low note. The right response to final presentations is praise and encouragement.

12

Visual aids

A student on one of my courses once gave a presentation on the construction of railways in Britain in the 19th century. It was well written and fluently delivered. But it used no visuals. Indeed it was like a radio script. As a result, I found myself frantically taking notes so that I could remember the many interesting points.

Almost without exception, lecturers use some form of visual communication even if it only consists of writing random headings or comments on a whiteboard. This chapter deals with pre-prepared visuals — their importance and how to design and produce them.

The need for visuals

Good visuals confer many benefits:

- Variety
- Retention
- Impact
- Signposting
- Clarity
- Conciseness
- Quality
- Consistency

Variety
The most persuasive reason for using visuals is that the spoken word engages only half of the listener's brain — the left hemisphere. Our left brain is analytical, recognizing and interpreting words, performing calculations. The words that you are reading at this moment are being processed by the left side of the brain. The right brain is the holistic, creative, artistic side. It takes in visual information — such as recognizing someone's face, understanding a diagram — in chunks. By using visuals we appeal to the visual, as well as the auditory, sense. The additional effectiveness of this as reinforcement has been confirmed by many studies.

Left and right brain thinking

Retention

Retention is closely bound up with the above. Much of our memory is photographic. When we search for something in a book we frequently know whereabouts on the page to look for it. Most feats of memory are visually-related. The simplest of these — remembering lists of words and recalling them at random — involves first committing a master checklist, for example, gun, shoe, tree, door, hive, sticks, heaven, plate, wine, hen, to memory. Using this you can easily memorize items on a different list by associating them with their equivalent on your master list. In doing this you make as outlandish a visual connection as you can conjure

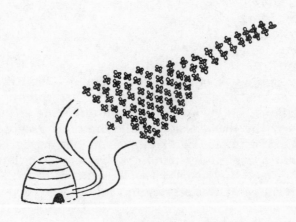

up. Suppose the fifth word in the new list is 'Concorde'; you could tie that to 'hive' by imagining a swarm of bees in such a shape.

The key to memory is association. Using this technique we make the image memorable by creating as unusual an association as possible. For longer-term retention we use a form of pattern recognition. One of the most impressive feats of memory was that of the Belgian grandmaster who played 55 simultaneous games of blindfold chess, winning 54 and drawing one! What is significant is that a chess player shown a chess board with the pieces randomly distributed has no better recall than anyone else. The ability to recall chess positions is associative, based on 'chunking' familiar patterns — white has castled on the king's side, black's queen is exposed and so on. To enable our students to recall over a longer term we need the association we create for them to be one that 'hooks onto' something that they are already closely familiar with.

Impact

Closely connected to retention is impact. A message may be given more effect, an attitude changed, a new angle given on a familiar topic, by judicious use of visual imagery. Figure 12.1 shows 'a new way of looking at the world'. Most of us are accustomed from birth to seeing maps with our own country in its familiar and rightful place as the centre of the known world. This altered view is in consequence visually arresting — it 'makes you think'. There is no reason why maps should show the

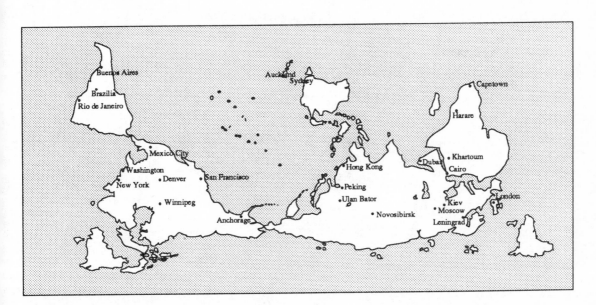

Figure 12.1   An Australian view of the world

Northern hemisphere at the top (with its connotations of supremacy); it just happens that the earliest cartographers were from the north and drew maps this way without ever thinking about it. This visual is an excellent example of how we can go about getting people to look at familiar things in a new light.

Signposting

This is the visual equivalent of telling people what we're going to say and then telling them what we've told them. If there is a structure to your lecture, it pays to let your audience in on the secret. The recipient of any communication is helped by an indication of what is coming, just as the message is reinforced by a summary of where he has been. Signposting can also deflect 'advance' questions, that is, those about topics we shall be covering later.

Signposting

Clarity

A picture paints a thousand words. Words are one-dimensional. The

".....for those of you unable to read......"

problem with the explanation of the 'Six Tables' diagram in Chapter 10 was that we were artificially forcing the use of narrative in a situation where the obvious solution was to draw a picture.

Conciseness

Closely linked to clarity is the ability of a picture to convey economically what it would take many words to say. This can be used to encapsulate important teaching points. The illustration shown below is a reminder to people giving presentations to:

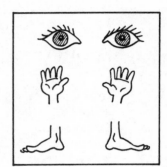

- Maintain eye contact

- Not let their hands wave aimlessly

- Stand erect.

Visuals reduce the amount of writing the presenter has to do. Whenever we write on a board or flipchart we risk the audience's attention wandering through loss of eye contact. This particularly applies to presenters with a penchant for writing theses rather than short, concise points.

Quality

The subconscious reaction to the problem in the above section is to write

.....the average lecturer's writing and drawing.

fast. This is in most cases synonymous with scribbling. Visuals can be thought out and produced at leisure. They will therefore be of a higher quality than the average lecturer's writing and drawing.

Consistency

Visuals are permanent and therefore have the advantage that they ensure that roughly the same thing is said each time the course is run. When the course is going to be run by a number of different presenters they enable the course writer to control the content of lectures and promote consistency between different presenters.

Thinking visually

In writing courseware it is important to think visually. I have had to school myself to do this because I am naturally a left side of the brain person. I am not alone in finding visualization difficult. When I succeed in persuading students of the need to use visuals it often results initially in words being transferred on to a slide. Words on visuals should be kept to a minimum. Wordy slides present the lecturer with a dilemma when he puts them up. Should he:

- Stand back and hum quietly to himself whilst the audience reads it?
- Read it out loud himself (with the implication that the audience cannot read)?
- Say something different from what is on the slide (giving his audience severe congestion of the left side of the brain)?

This problem does not arise if we keep visuals visual. The right side of the brain can take in the image; the left side can take in the lecturer's words. This is not to say that we have no words on visuals, merely that we keep them to the minimum necessary to make the point clear. A little imagination can usually find a more pictorial way of presenting ideas. The examples that follow — mind maps, visual analogies, balances, grids, graphs, cartoons — are illustrations of ways in which we can turn words into pictures.

Mind maps

Visuals written in straight linear, narrative mode are referred to in my company as 'left-brain slides'. If we need to represent ideas in some structure we can often do so in the form of a mind map. Mind maps are an alternative to, and usually an improvement on, indented lists. The syllabus of the 'Training the Trainers' course could be represented as shown in Figure 12.2. Is shows the structure of the course more clearly than a list arranged into headings, sub-headings and sub-sub-headings.

It also gives us the opportunity to cross-connect items as when a process such as video-recording is being used at different points throughout the course. However, it contains a lot of words and an illustration of this type is more suited to the course manual than overhead projection.

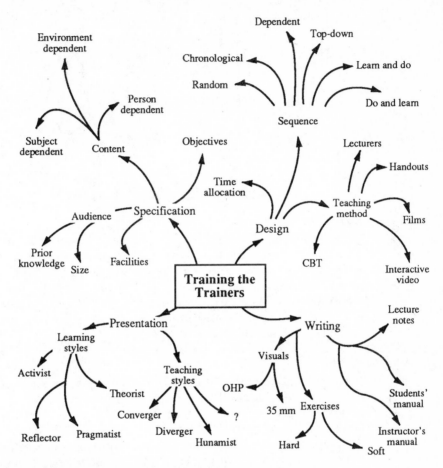

Figure 12.2 Mind map for Training the Trainers

Visual analogies

A little thought can often provide us with a visual representation of a concept that we are trying to communicate. Many signs — particularly those used internationally — use symbols instead of words. An idle way of passing away time in airport lounges and other similar places is to observe the many different pictures used to depict the difference between male and female lavatories. My current collection includes, among others, trousers/skirts, roosters/hens, low-heeled/high-heeled shoes, knights and ladies.

Non-gender-specific signs

Balances

Often when teaching soft topics we need to convey the idea of a trade-off between two variables, where more of one entails less of the other — what is known as a 'zero-sum game'. When I said in Chapter 9 that the more complex a technique, the simpler should be any illustrative material, this was an example of such a trade-off. For most of us, leisure is a trade-off against earning more money. Such relationships can be depicted as a set of scales.

Grids

A trade-off means that more of one item entails correspondingly less of the other — dependent variables. However, in other circumstances, variables may be independent of each other — you can have more or less of either or both. Blake's and Mouton's Managerial Grid represents management styles as a mixture of people and task orientation. Increasing the people skills of the managers does not need to be at the price of their ability to get things done; the two variables move independently of each other. The great advantage of such a diagram is that it requires a minimum of words. The lecturer can then develop the theme, adding the words to the diagram if he so wishes. This gives a good mixture between what is said and what is seen. (See Figure 12.3.) The Grid is derived from a study of different management styles and situations. These have then been analysed into main components of people-orientation and task-orientation. The Grid expresses this analysis, adding a touch of visual authenticity. Blake offers a laboratory learning experience in which participants gain feedback from others as to where they fall on the Grid. Then they can follow guidelines to improve their style of management. Blake is hardening up management.

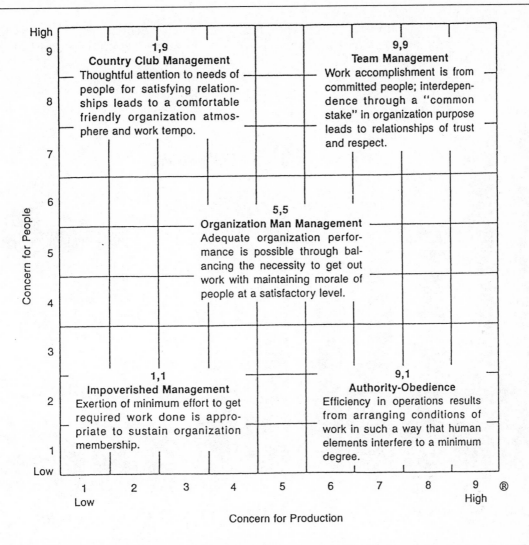

Source: The Managerial Grid figure from *The Managerial Grid III: The Key to Leadership Excellence* by Robert R. Blake and Jane Srygley Mouton. Houston: Gulf Publishing Company, Copyright © 1985, page 12. Reproduced by permission.

Figure 12.3   The Managerial Grid®

Graphs

There is a great variety of different types of graphs that one can draw. Giving this term its widest meaning, one can identify histograms, pie-charts and many other devices without their own names. Figure 12.4 illustrates a histogram showing the exports from Dubai between 1971 and 1981. What makes this a particularly striking example is that at first sight it appears to be showing a disastrous decline. In fact it is the reverse; Arabic histograms, like Arabic writing, but unlike numerals, go from right to left!

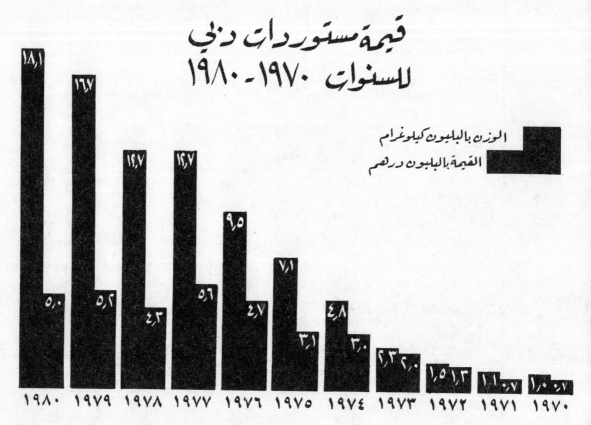

Figure 12.4   Histogram of Dubai exports 1971–1981

Cartoons

Cartoons are a good opportunity to lighten a session, and reinforce a teaching point, with humour. Not everyone has the good fortune to be able to call on the talents of an illustrator as with this book. Nevertheless, much can be done with a bit of cut and paste. You should, however, be wary of breaching copyright.

Production of visuals

So much for thinking visually. The next step is to transfer our ideas on to visuals. The key questions here are:

- How many visuals should we use per lecture session?
- Is there any rule which dictates how much information one visual should contain?

How many per session?

Some subjects, particularly hard ones, are more conducive to visuals than others; some lecturers are more at home with visuals than others; one can even make it environment-dependent by saying that some audiences expect visual presentations more than others, or that lecturers have different levels of technology available for their preparation.

The harder a topic is, the more it benefits from pre-prepared visuals. In hard topics the relationship between teacher and student is closer to parent-child in terms of the relative knowledge that each side has (although, hopefully, not in terms of how the material is presented). The teacher has greater control of the material; the session is less a dialogue. It is more structured, more predictable.

Soft teaching works on the assumption that the audience has more to contribute. One is looking for participants to come to conclusions for themselves rather than have them dictated by the lecturer. This process never gets off the ground if the lecturer inhibits discussion with a series of pre-prepared visuals.

Consequently, for some sessions I have no pre-prepared visuals. I pose a question 'What makes a good manager?' and write the answers up as they emerge. I personally am happiest when lecturing in this mode. However, it is something of a confidence trick. Hardening up the course has forced me to come up with my own list. It is made available as a handout after the session with an accompanying commentary. Fortunately, most of my audiences see good managers the same way that I do!

How much information on each?

If I were forced to set a 'pseudo-hard' rule I would say: 'No more than twenty words'. But it is impossible to lay down a general rule. So much depends on what one is teaching. An 'impact' visual will have few words and a strong visual message. Informative visuals would usually contain more. A list of topics, or mind map, could well contain seven or eight entries; a complex diagram might, perforce, have to descend to a fair level of detail.

I find it constructive to talk in terms of a minimum and maximum amount of time that the lecturer intends to devote to a visual. A simple rule of thumb is: *Always leave yourself something to say*. This has to be thought about at the time of designing the visual. By the time you put up a visual with six headings, each with four lines of writing, it is too late. All you can do is cover half of it up. Am I alone in objecting to people who put up a slide only immediately to hide it from me? I am always more interested in what I am not being shown rather than what I am.

143

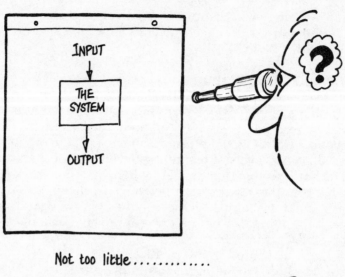

Not too little..............

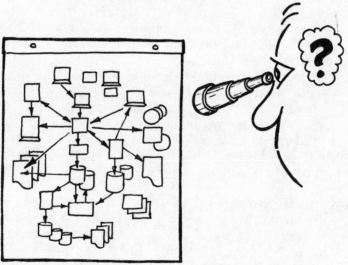

Not too much...............

Build them up, don't cover them up

Quite often a fair amount of information is required on a visual. The best solution in this case is to build up the visual by overlays turning the one slide into three or four and superimposing them on each other as you proceed. This looks professional and can be very effective. This 'build-up' process is even easier and more effective with 35-mm slides where each succeeding slide has one more item added to its predecessor. Occasionally the presenter may want to draw directly on to prepared slides (one reason why I prefer OHPs to 35mm). In this case it is better

144

to protect the slide by placing a blank foil on top of it and drawing on that.

For informative visuals I put forward a guideline of display of between 30 seconds and two minutes each. Below this, there is a risk of confusing the audience with the blur of hands as they are put on and off; above this and there is probably too much information being displayed at a time. The 'top-down' sequence should be considered as a means of turning one complex visual into three simpler ones.

What about the physical process of producing the visuals? In writing this book I have drawn on the services of a professional illustrator. Obviously, this option is not within everyone's budget when course writing. In this case you are dependent on your own talents and the technology you have available to you. The latter will dictate the mechanics of visual production and to a large extent the quality of the finished product.

Tracing/photocopying

Overhead projector (OHP) slides are often referred to as transparencies for the very good reason that you can see through them. This means that we can put lined paper underneath them to keep our writing straight or we can trace a picture directly from an original. Books are available whose purchase entitles you to reproduce the illustrations in them — of anything from *The Wreck of the Hesperus* to Rodin's *Thinker* (both of which have their use in courses on systems development). Almost all modern photocopiers have the facility of making copies direct on to transparencies. This does away with the necessity of tracing and enables more complex diagrams to be prepared manually, or by computer, and transferred on to slides.

Computer graphics

All the words and many of the illustrations in this book were produced on my personal computer. In addition to using programs to originate diagrams, you can obtain a library of ready-drawn pictures which you can cut and paste, crop, amend and generally play around with to your heart's content.

I once gave a paper at a conference on systems methodologies. In my talk I used the common metaphor of a 'chicken and egg situation'. I asked a colleague to make up an illustration for me using his graphics disk. He rang me to say that my assumption that his disk contained a chicken was correct. The only problem was that it was a roast chicken. The resulting slide gave an unplanned touch of humour in a conference which was otherwise short of laughs.

From my experience of watching presentations on courses I know that the quality of visuals is a prime influence in getting a message across.

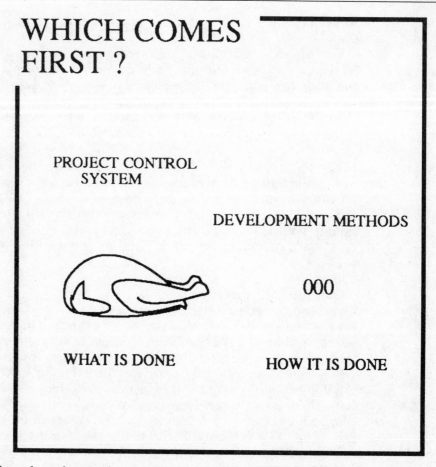

WHICH COMES FIRST ?

PROJECT CONTROL
SYSTEM

DEVELOPMENT METHODS

000

WHAT IS DONE

HOW IT IS DONE

Often the solution that impresses most is not that which is best designed, but that which is best presented. Do everything you can to ensure that you have the appropriate technology at your disposal.

Integrating visuals and text

The student manual

Visuals displayed by the presenter are an obvious example of non-permanent communication — with the possible exception of an impact slide that is engraved on the student's memory for ever. It is sensible, therefore, to consider whether copies of visuals should be included in any handout. In compiling a student's manual the course writer will be guided first by any standards current within his company. If none exist, he can choose a format with which he is most comfortable. There are many different attitudes to the form a student manual should take. Among those that I have seen are:

- Copies of slides used by the lecturers
- A series of checklists, mainly for use after the course
- A transcript of the lectures
- Examples of model solutions to class exercises
- Published books on the relevant subject
- Any combination of the above.

After some years of experimenting with a variety of approaches, my own company standardized on a format which combines a copy of the lecturer's visual with a commentary on the facing page. This obviates copious note-taking and enables students to link the manual back to the lecture through the slides. For the student, the visual element improves retention; for the course writer, the standard has the effect of forcing him to think visually, drafting the visual aids first and then writing the commentary round them.

One must not be dogmatic about this precise format. A one-to-one relationship between visuals and text is not always convenient. But the adoption of this as a standard has hardened up my own course writing by imposing a clear and consistent discipline on the format of the manual. A visual is expected to make one specific point; the point is then expanded and documented on the facing page. Adherence to this standard makes the course more readily transportable between instructors. A first-draft presenter's guide can be produced by dictating, page by page, an expanded version of the commentary including any examples, anecdotes, questions and other embellishments that are not in the manual.

Another approach is to provide a pocket-sized guide. This is typically printed on card and is designed as an *aide-mémoire* for the student, picking out the major rules, guidelines or techniques taught on the course. The format is designed to maximize the probability of his making use of it. (For example see Figure 12.5)

Scriptboard

Before investigating the large amount of time needed to put together a students' manual we need another review. The course writer therefore creates a 'scriptboard'. This is a detailed guide to each of the sessions. The format of visuals plus commentary is a very convenient layout from which to review the courseware. Part of the scriptboard for the 'Training the Trainers' course might be as shown in Figure 12.6.

This format greatly facilitates quality assurance. Once the scriptboard has been approved, the writer can complete the detailed writing of the course, including the presenter's guide. The resulting end-product should be well-documented, prescriptive enough to ensure that when run by different presenters it remains the same course, whilst allowing some flexibility for individual presenters to put their own stamp on it.

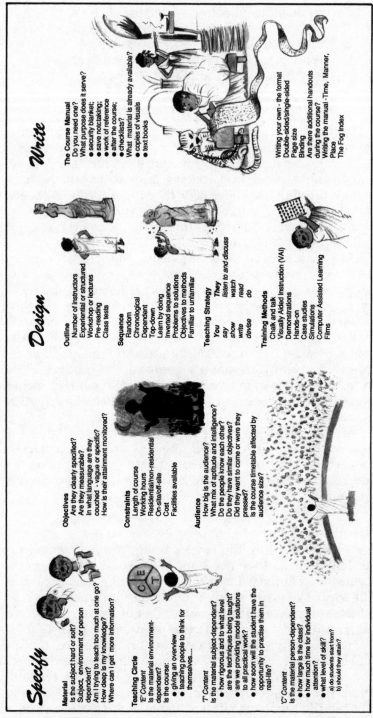

Figure 12.5 Trainers' guide

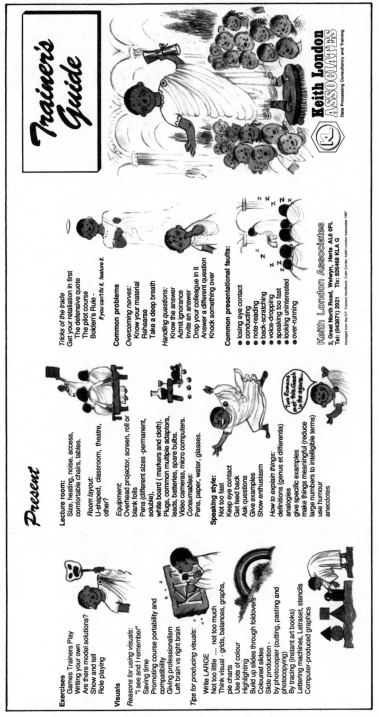

Figure 12.5   Trainers' guide *concluded*

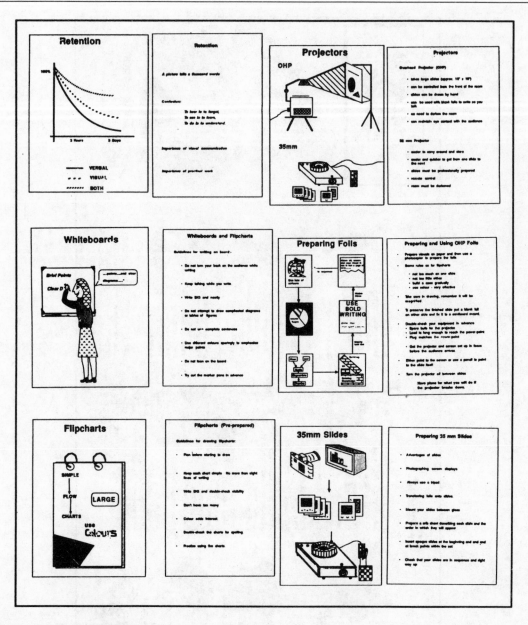

Figure 12.6 Scriptboard

Part IV
Presenting the course

Good course design and writing are necessary conditions of effective teaching. But they are not sufficient conditions. That is, there is no course written that a bad presenter cannot ruin (though there are plenty of badly-written courses that a good presenter can go a long way to overcome).

The presenter must have:

- Complete grasp of the subject matter of the course
- Expertise in presentation and teaching techniques
- Ability to manage a participative learning experience
- Ability to motivate students.

Course presenters are like waiters in that they are in the direct firing line for problems (in their case, of design and writing) which may not be of their making. Conversely, the success of a course is also going to be laid at their door, irrespective of whether it owes more to the designer and writer. They should therefore take a keen interest in the courseware they are teaching as well as in the techniques for presenting it.

To what extent are the skills of presentation person-dependent? Are good presenters born or made? The intention of the following two chapters is to 'harden up' presentational skills by identifying the things that good presenters *do* (as opposed to the qualities they possess). But there is one rule that goes a long way to answering the 'born or made' question: *The secret of spontaneity is careful presentation.* The presenter, whose silver tongue you so admire, was not born like that. He has taken the trouble to organise his thoughts, know his material and research the answers to any questions that may previously have floored him.

13

On your hind legs

The secret of professionalism in any discipline lies in operating comfortably within one's level of competence. Most stage musicians give the appearance of playing relatively non-complex chord sequences not that far removed from amateur rock groups. The difference is that the latter are at the limits of their ability, whilst the professional musician has plenty in hand. The two 'Ps' — preparation and practice — bring about the desired teaching state of knowing a lot more about a subject than you have time to impart. The common analogy to fix this in people's minds is that of an iceberg. An iceberg has the greater part of its mass

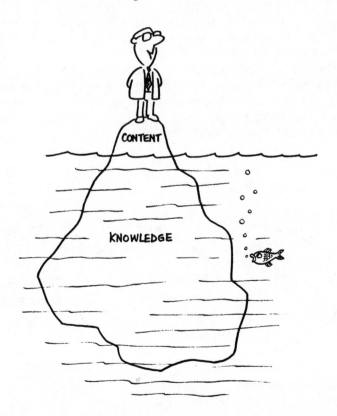

below the visible line. If the iceberg represents the totality of our knowledge of a subject, what we make visible is the content of our prepared lectures. The remaining knowledge is there to enable us to answer questions. Were we to ban all questions we would not need the iceberg. Imagine you are taking a history exam. You are fortunate enough to have been given a prior look at the exam paper. Knowing what questions are going to be asked would eliminate a vast amount of work. You would just prepare the answers to however many questions you have to complete. It is because students do not have prior knowledge of exam papers that they have to spend two years studying in order to write three hours' worth of answers. Consider that as a ratio of knowledge possessed to knowledge displayed. Then apply the same ratio to lectures. A knowledge of what you will be asked in advance makes life easy. Without it we just have to 'over-prepare'. For hard courses this means in-depth knowledge of facts, figures and techniques; for soft courses it means awareness of the pros and cons of different approaches in different situations and for different people.

It is vital that the presenter can quickly establish his credibility as a teacher. How is this done? Obviously by a demonstrable mastery of what he is talking about. But this is a lot easier to demonstrate on hard courses than soft ones. In the latter we are asking people to accept certain views rather than clearly demonstrable facts. Why should our students believe us? What credentials do we have for imposing our views? One way is by establishing our knowledge and judgement in different areas first. The two sets shown in Figure 13.1 represent what we each know about the world. The important area is the intersection of the sets — things that we both know. In the non-intersecting areas it is impossible for us to validate each other's knowledge or opinions. We therefore inevitably tend to judge people on their knowledge of, or attitudes towards, things that we ourselves know about.

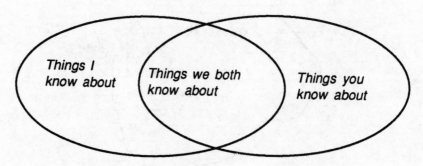

Figure 13.1 Knowledge sets

Suppose that you have just sat through a session on leadership styles. The lecturer sounded convincing, but while talking informally outside the lecture room you discover that he talks just as authoritatively about the American system of government, the geography of Outer Mongolia and the marriage customs of the Hottentots — in one of which subjects you just happen to be expert. You suddenly realize that he is talking a load of impressive-sounding nonsense. It would not be long before you made the connection that perhaps his views on leadership were in the same class. You have extrapolated, with good reason, from subjects that you know about to subjects in which you are ignorant. The result is that the lecturer has lost his credibility.

The converse is also true, as I demonstrated on a student who had just visited Disneyworld. She waxed eloquent about the realistic representations of villages from all over the world — English, Thai, Masai and so on — praising the attention to detail. 'You've been to Kenya?' I asked innocently. 'No,' she replied, wondering what was coming. 'But you said the Masai village was perfect in every detail . . . .' 'Oh, well, I haven't actually seen a Masai village in real life, but it looked very realistic.' 'Thailand?' 'Actually I've never been there either but the English village was certainly right in every detail.' She had extrapolated from the one area that she knew about to those where she did not and had drawn the obvious conclusion that if Disneyworld went to the trouble to get the English village correct it was likely that the others were as well. We need students to draw the conclusion that since we talk sense about subjects they are familiar with, we are also talking sense when we put forward the ideas that form the subject matter of the course and with which they are less familiar.

Motivation

Motivation is the key to successful teaching. Although at school, teachers may drum Latin conjugations into unwilling students, once schooldays are over learning is largely a voluntary affair. Unfortunately a teacher cannot flick a switch to guarantee a highly-motivated course any more than he can make a New Year's resolution to be happy. Motivation, like happiness, is the by-product of things happening in a certain way. This is not to say that you cannot set out to achieve a high level of motivation just as you can set out personal goals which you will find happiness in achieving; what it means is that motivation is not something that you can pick up off the shelf, as you can a training aid in order to add variety. Motivation is an on-going task. It is making people want to learn.

We all hope that our students come with a desire to learn. If they are not motivated at the outset we need to inspire them; if they start motivated we need to ensure that they stay that way. As we have seen, a large part of this depends on how the course is written. But the presenter still must work hard at encouraging participation and at making a subject come alive. Making a subject come alive is the single greatest contribution a teacher can make. In so doing his influence long outlasts the classroom.

What motivates people

One of the most useful contributions to the theory of motivation is Herzberg's research into what people see as motivating and demotivating factors in their work.[1] Herzberg used the term 'motivators' and 'hygiene factors.' Motivators are what encourage people to work — they relate mainly to the *content* of work: achievement, recognition, responsibility. Hygiene factors — company policy, working conditions, salary — relate to the *context* within which the job is carried out. They cannot of themselves act as motivators but they may demotivate if unsatisfactory.

In recent years I have conducted my own survey among students on my courses as to what they consider to be motivating and demotivating factors in training. Based on this research, and using Herzberg's terms, hygiene factors in a learning environment are:

- Space, temperature and external noise level in the lecture room
- Freedom from interruption
- Good food — the right amount and good quality
- Plenty of good hot coffee/tea at break times
- Breaks taken out of the lecture room
- The hours and duration of the course
- A high standard of accommodation for a residential course.

Note that, mirroring Herzberg's findings, these relate almost exclusively to the course context or setting. Those factors that show up as motivators on courses — and which mostly reflect the content, including presentation — are:

- Relevance of the subject matter
- The right degree of challenge
- The feeling that one is making progress
- Variation of training methods on the course
- The instructor's own enthusiasm for the subject
- Treatment of students as individuals
- Creation, and maintenance, of a positive course attitude by attention to the social as well as learning aspects of the course
- The feeling that learning is a pleasant activity.

Note that, of these, four are connected with how the course was developed, four with how it is given. I believe the last item in the list to be the most important. Before any sense data gets to the processing part of the brain it must pass through the thalamus which controls our feelings, notably of pleasure and displeasure. All information processed by the brain therefore involves some sort of feelings. Experiments have shown that when the feelings associated with learning are unpleasant, less is retained than when they are pleasant. Thus it is vital that we make learning an enjoyable experience both by the variety and interest of the work and by judicious use of praise and encouragement.

The last aspect is of particular importance. In an experiment conducted by Rosenthal,[2] a class of students was randomly divided into three groups. Their teachers were led to believe that they had been grouped according to ability. After six months the progress of the groups was measured. The A group, perceived by the teachers as being the brightest group, had made significantly more progress than the B group, which in turn had out-performed the C group. It appears from this that learning is closely correlated with the teacher's expectations. We should approach our task with an air of confidence that students will learn. Such an attitude goes a long way to being self-fulfilling.

Given this general picture of motivation, what specific guidelines and tips can we devise to increase motivation on a course?

1. First be aware of whether or not people are motivated. Many people are too polite to tell you if they are finding the course unrewarding. You must be alert to body language or actively seek out feedback.
2. Always think of the course from the learner's standpoint. Too often we concentrate on those aspects of the material of most interest to ourselves, use anecdotes about experiences that are of consuming interest to us but less so to the students.
3. Do not let discontent or apathy fester. If you become aware of someone who is not motivated, discuss it with him. If the whole class is in a state of educational lassitude, discuss it with them. This hurts and therefore demands a lot of self-confidence on the part of the presenter. But it has to be done. The alternative of soldiering on and vaguely hoping that things will get better seldom does any good.
4. Enthusiasm and apathy are equally contagious. If your body-language (hopefully not your spoken language) says 'I wish I were somewhere else', your students will rapidly come round to your way of thinking.
5. Treat students as individuals:

   - Learn and remember their names
   - Find a common interest such as a colleague from the same department or company
   - Foster group harmony
   - Draw out the reticent
   - Encourage those lacking in self-confidence
   - Help anyone who gets stuck

- Protect the shy
- Channel the energies of the enthusiast.

Before the course

Engendering the right learning environment starts before the course. Delegates will normally receive some prior information, typically joining instructions. This is a good opportunity to say something about the nature of the course and how they can get the most benefit from it. It can be an opportunity for the presenter to learn in advance about delegates by the inclusion of a questionnaire. In some instances, some work can be assigned in advance. Least successful is when the latter is pre-reading; best is when a specific task is given. On the 'Training the Trainers' course we ask delegates to come prepared to give a ten-minute presentation. This will assuredly get done, because no one wants to make a fool of themselves in front of a class; it has the added benefit of shifting preparation time out of valuable course time. The presenter should think about the first meeting with delegates. People are nervous of first encounters and it is the presenter's job to put them at their ease. This may be little more than having coffee served immediately before the course starts or a drink at the bar where a residential course checks in on the preceding evening. This aspect is very environment-dependent; it depends on the type of course, whether it is in-company or external, whether some or all of the delegates know each other. But it sets the tone for the course. On the technical leadership course mentioned in Chapter 10 delegates are deliberately not greeted by the course presenter. They are given an envelope containing instructions on sorting themselves out into teams. This approach is consistent with the type of course, immediately demonstrating that they will be expected to think for themselves during the coming week.

Room set-up

My motivation survey highlighted the importance of the physical learning environment. I shall assume that this has resulted in your having a large, airy, quiet room in which to lecture. What is under the presenter's control is how it is set up. Just as first greeting can influence how a course is run, so can the layout of the lecture room. How do we want our audience to be seated relative to each other and the presenter? Let us revert to our schooldays. Why are school classrooms laid out in rows with the desks one behind another? There are two answers to this question, both of which are relevant to how we set up our own lecture room. The first is simple: the constraints of class size against number of students. Even if the teacher wanted the desks to be in a horseshoe, lack of space would prevent it.

The second reason is to do with teaching style. At school most teaching, at least until sixth form, is hard. The teacher knows the answers and communicates these to the students. Interaction tends to be between teacher and students rather than from student to student. This reflects an implicit attitude that students have little to learn from each other — which is far from the truth when running soft courses for adults.

Within a university environment this changes. With the exception of lectures (which are one-way communication often of the worst teaching kind) classes are smaller, seats are more comfortable; at the older universities you may even be given a sherry. The environment is made conducive to the flow of ideas and interchange of opinion.

We see from this that room set-up needs careful thought. We can weigh up the most common possibilities using our subject/environment/person-dependent analysis. Room set-up is environment-dependent in terms of space, sight-lines, equipment needed, size of audience, and person-dependent in terms of the relationship the teacher wants to establish between himself and the students. Different set-ups can be as follows:

1. Classroom-style — inhibits interaction between the students. Suitable mainly for hard courses.
2. Herringbone — a compromise between classroom and a more open arrangement when numbers preclude the latter.
3. Horseshoe ('U') — the most usual set-up for interactive teaching. It enables students to see each other as well as the teacher. Sight lines to the screen can be improved by opening the 'U' into more of a 'V'.
4. Group tables — used occasionally on workshop courses when a group needs to stay together during lecture sessions.

When setting up a room for my own courses I ensure that my own table is so positioned that I can easily get 'class-side' of it and so reduce barriers between me and the audience. On some courses I go as far as making the set-up almost circular as a means of reducing the difference in status between me and the delegates. I am keen to establish what is known in Transactional Analysis as an 'adult-adult' relationship which is the opposite of conventional school teaching where the teacher likes to reinforce his authority by adopting a parent-child relationship. But then school teachers have discipline and motivation problems unknown to most commercial trainers!

Teaching styles

I once gave a two-day course on microcomputers to an audience of senior managers drawn from a large multinational. This was a pilot course and students' reactions were closely monitored. When I rang the training manager he said that the course reviews were unlike any he had seen before. I trembled in anticipation. Had I committed the worst disaster, or run the best course, of my career? He went on to explain that what was unusual was the widest diversity of any reviews he had ever seen. Comments ranged from 'truly excellent course', 'best I've ever attended', 'tremendous lecturer', to 'didn't understand a word of it', 'we won't be wanting this course in our branch'.

We saw, in Chapter 5, that students have their own preferred learning styles. Teachers too have their preferred teaching styles and question-naires exist which identify these styles. The following, by Richard Brostrom, invites you to assign marks for responses such as those shown below on a scale of one to four:

1. The purpose of training should be:

   - To develop the participants' competency and mastery of specific skills
   - To transfer needed information to the learner in the most efficient way
   - To establish the learner's capacity to solve his or her own problems
   - To facilitate certain insights on the part of the participants.

2. Teaching methods

   - Should be relatively flexible but present real challenges to the learner
   - Should be determined by the subject
   - Must emphasize trial and feedback
   - Must allow freedom for the individual learner.

From answers to these it categorizes teaching styles in terms of one's views of how people learn — see Figure 13.2. An analysis is given below of the strengths and limitations of the different teaching styles.

1. *Behaviourist*   Strengths — the 'doctor': clear, precise, complete security, trust builder, in control.
   Limitations — The 'manipulator': fosters dependence, overprotective, withholds data.
2. *Structuralist*   Strengths — the 'expert': informative, thorough, systematic, good audio-visual techniques, strong leader, well-rehearsed, entertaining.
   Limitations — the 'Elitist': preoccupied with means rather than results, inflexible, black-and-white thinking, superior.
3. *Functionalist*   Strengths — the 'coach': emphasizes purpose, takes risks, gives feedback, builds confidence.

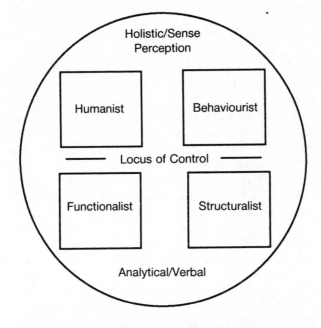

People deal with wholes, not parts — intuitively, emotionally, physically. They move spontaneously, unpredictably, unconsciously, non-linearly (right-brain activity)

Holistic/Sense Perception

Humanist

Behaviourist

People prefer independence, autonomy, and the chance to control their own destinies; they are internally directed

Locus of Control

People respond to forces around them. They prefer guidance from others or the environment; they are externally directed

Functionalist

Structuralist

Analytical/Verbal

People's minds work rationally, intellectually, scientifically. Information is processed systematically, sequentially, for storage (memory) and retrieval (left-brain activity)

Figure 13.2   Teaching style matrix

       Limitations — 'sink or swim': intimidating, competitive, overly task-oriented.

4.   *Humanist*   Strengths — the 'counsellor': sensitive, open, spontaneous, facilitative, interactive, responsive to learners.
       Limitations — the 'fuzzy thinker': abstract, unconcerned with time, poor control of group, resists 'teaching', appears unprepared.

I have found that this test produces an accurate and invaluable insight into my own teaching style and those of my colleagues. It can be seen as the extension of the hard/soft analysis applied to teachers and analysed in considerable detail. If we choose to stay with our strengths we will gravitate towards the type of courses where our approach is most appropriate. By concentrating on improving the areas of the limitations of our style we can better cope with all teaching situations.

Running the course

Introductions

It is customary for the lecturer to introduce himself and then get the delegates to do the same. A variation is to get students to interview and then introduce each other. I do not personally do this because I want to hear what individuals have to say about themselves in their own words, particularly their objectives in coming on the course. As mentioned above, one modification is to send delegates a short questionnaire about their work experience. This is mainly to help in assigning syndicates and exercises. But the questionnaire also asks for personal information such as interests outside work. Replies are then word-processed prior to the course and form part of the initial course handout. It is a good ice-breaker for people who are often nervous at the start of a course and need to be brought out. Without this, two dedicated antiquarians could easily go the whole week without discovering their shared interest.

The most important point about introductions is — keep them short. In this the lecturer should lead by example, resisting the common temptation to tell his life history under the pretext of establishing his credibility. In checking delegates' objectives in coming on the course be careful how you phrase the question. I used to put it in the form, 'Why are you here?'. Apart from occasionally eliciting the annoying but useful answer 'I don't know' this is an open invitation to the wag of the class. Among the answers I have received over the years are:

- We had £300 left in our training budget which we had to spend before year-end. (civil servant)
- I'm here to listen to what you're telling them. (DP manager accompanying three users on an introductory computer course)
- I am semi-retired and like to spend part of my year in London. I love your theatre and opera but find myself at a loose end during the daytime so I thought I'd learn something about computers. (South American millionaire, aged 72)

Other items that should form part of the initial introductory session are administrative details such as meal-times, procedures for taking messages, and so on. The introductory session is a chance to overcome students' fears about talking in front of the rest of the group. It can also set the tone for the participation that the lecturer wants to encourage.

Establishing rapport

It is most important that a teacher, early on in the course, gets onto the same wavelength as his audience. As we have seen, students' attitudes differ widely. Some are there because they have been told to come rather than volunteering. Others may harbour a concealed grudge against salesmen, industrial psychologists, computer specialists, or whatever work-group you happen to represent. It is important to establish that you can put yourself in their shoes. It is no use merely saying it, you have to demonstrate it. One of the ways that I used to do this on a computing course for non-computing people was to state early on that one of the problems in computing is the vast amount of jargon that surrounds it (a proposition I can be confident will command their assent). I would then put up a slide containing the following sentence: 'DPPX/BASE licence program is a multi-programming communications-oriented operating system for use in a distributed data processing environment'. Having read through it I would inform them, tongue in cheek, that by the end of the course expressions such as these would be 'tripping off their tongue' and they would be 'the envy of their friends at dinner parties'. The implied criticism of the industry's jargon immediately persuaded my audience that I was on their side.

Encouraging audience participation

Suppose you have to stand in at short notice for a colleague and give an hour's lecture. You know very little about the subject but you have been given a full set of lecture notes and visuals; sufficiently complete, in fact, for you virtually to be able to read them out verbatim and thus fill the hour. Your worry is that someone might ask you a question, as you would almost certainly not be able to answer it. What would you do to inhibit audience participation without actually telling them? My guess is that consciously or subconsciously you would:

.... *positioning yourself behind a lectern.*

163

- Use discouraging body language, such as positioning yourself behind a lectern
- Speak fast in order not to leave gaps where people could ask questions
- Avoid eye contact with the audience as much as possible.

What you are doing is *controlling* your audience, albeit to a negative end. Audience control is important and participation carries the ever-present risk of loss of control. Someone may ask a question to which you do not know the answer or which relates to a topic you intend to cover at a different time; a student may disagree with a point you have made; a discussion breaks out that puts you behind the clock; the course bore may take the floor.

Nevertheless these are dangers we must face and learn to overcome. Because without participation we have no measure of whether we are communicating or not. Feedback is vital when we are lecturing in dependency sequence; it is equally essential when we are teaching soft topics where our objective is to stimulate our students to think for themselves.

The above example was designed to make clear that achieving audience participation is not simply a matter of throwing the occasional question at them. We should adopt the reverse of the behaviour patterns noted above as a prerequisite of fostering participation. It should then come spontaneously. Beyond that we can deliberately ask for it. Instead of the parent-child approach: 'Here are the six rules for . . .', pose it as a question: 'What in your opinion are the characteristics of a good manager . . . typical problems of systems development . . .?' (But have your own answers at the ready and know what you will do if nobody offers anything or if their analysis differs from yours!) This last point is significant. I repeat: all forms of participative learning carry the ever-present threat of loss of control. Participants may put forward, and rigorously defend, answers which do not match your own; the audience may collectively be struck dumb. I have been reduced to begging for a response before now! Often there is a concealed dependency in this form of interaction. Having asked my audience for their view of the problems of systems development my next visual in the above sequence is of the solutions to the problems. If my audience comes up with a completely different list of problems from mine they will not go much on my solutions. Sometimes some discreet guidance is necessary to get the right answer!

Humour

About the only advantage that Walter Mondale, the Democratic candidate, had over Ronald Reagan in the 1984 US presidential election was the latter's age. The question was being continually asked: 'Wasn't Reagan too old to serve a second term?' Notice the predictability of the question. When questions are known in advance you do not need to possess a quick mind to make a snappy reply — you can prepare one. In this instance, to be precise, the speechwriters could. In the second television debate between the two candidates the question came up: 'Mr President, would you not agree that age is an issue in this election?' This time the response was ready. 'I'm not going to exploit for political purposes my opponent's youth and inexperience.' Roger Ailes, Reagan's media consultant, claims that this was the moment when the election was won.

The moral is that humour is one of the communicator's most potent weapons. It can be used to make lectures more interesting, to recover from a disaster, or to take the sting out of a personality clash. Humour is person-dependent* in both the teller and the receiver. Some lecturers have stock jokes built into their lectures. Others have an apparently inexhaustible supply in their head any of which might be triggered spontaneously by a student's remark. As with all devices it suffers from the law of diminishing returns. People enjoy a laugh but it is possible to have too much of a good thing.

"You're going to love this one."

*Having said that I did once try to harden up humour as a result of being roped in to help with the writing of a revue. It is an interesting exercise which can be carried out by the process described in Chapter 9. To get you started, step 2 (Identify the Technique) reveals various types — *the double entendre* (simple and extended — the basis of most dirty jokes); the satiric (*Spitting Images*); the unexpected (most situation comedies); the predictable looming disaster (Basil Fawlty); the put-down (Australian); the off-beat (Ministry of Silly Walks); the exaggerated (dead parrot).

165

Anecdotes

These are stories — usually based on fact, improved with the telling — which lecturers use to illustrate and reinforce teaching points. Often they will be humorous, sometimes cautionary; always they must be relevant. Their purpose should be to increase student's understanding and retention by reinforcing a point with a specific illustration. If we wish to persuade people of the necessity of agreeing a specification before starting design we relate how company X failed to do this and wrote off a million pounds in development work that had to be scrapped.

I am always alert for new tips, amusing anecdotes, better analogies and so on. Many of these I pick up from students on my courses who in the important sessions at the bar relate disaster stories of such horrendous proportions and such intrinsic amusement that one knows immediately that they will regale generations of students yet unborn. I always found the testing of computer systems to be an egregiously boring topic. This all changed when one of my students told me about the pharmaceutical benefits system in Australia where a program bug eluded some hurried system testing caused by the project being behind schedule. The bug was discovered four years later — by which time it had cost the Australian government $253 million in over-payment to pharmacists. It is such an excellent example that the only question is one of sequence — whether you hit people with it at the start of a session in order to get their attention, or use it at the end as a means of finishing on a high note.

Tricks of the trade

The 'next time list'

We have all suffered the frustration of thinking up a telling or amusing answer to a question two hours after fumbling for one in a lecture. (Indeed many languages have a colloquial expression for just this situation.) There is not much that one can do about this if the lecture was a one-off. However, most lectures are repeat performances. Provided you write down the witty quip that occurs to you too late, you can incorporate this into your notes for the next occasion.

Often such points occur during a lecture or exercise. They may be the direct result of a problem with an exercise — perhaps a briefing note needs rewriting. On my 'Training the Trainers' course I ostentatiously stick up a sheet of flipchart paper headed 'Colin's Next Time List'. Whenever anyone finds a bug in the course — the need for a hole-punch, a better map of how to get to the hotel — I write it down on my list. By extolling the benefits of such a list, and giving a practical demonstration, I persuade my students that they are learning something of great value whenever they run across something else that I have forgotten. This is a classic use of Bolden's rule which states:

'If you can't fix it, feature it.'

The best-laid plans gang oft aglay. It is no good adopting an apologetic air and drawing attention to the problems. You have to make a virtue of it. If the lecture room is too small, emphasize how intimate it is; if the ink is still wet on your handouts, draw attention to how up-to-date the material is; if your carefully-prepared demonstration crashes, point out how life-like your courses are — they can see how an experienced presenter handles a disaster!

"..... So we've tried to create an environment in which interpersonal skills can be developed and tested."

The useful quote

Quotations show that you are not the first person to have thought a particular thought. They lend a kind of legitimacy to views and opinions, always welcome when soft teaching. Or they can be used to 'put down' a troublesome student. Are you having trouble with someone who knows it all, who has nothing to learn from your course? Try Francis Bacon:

> If you start with certainties you will end with doubt; but if you are content to start with doubts, you will end in certainties. *Advancement of Learning*.

On one of my courses there was a young woman who was having to teach an electronic office system to secretaries twice her age and ten times her secretarial experience. But she was the expert on this particular system. It is quite usual for us to find ourselves teaching skills to people

167

who have been 'in the field' longer, or more recently, than we have. However, many people can do the same job for years without any discernible improvement. Content yourself with Thomas Hardy's phrase:

Experience is as to intensity, not to duration.

If you feel defensive about a case study on the basis that no real-life company could be that stupid (they almost certainly could), you should use Coleridge's phrase:

The suspension of disbelief.

The pilot course

We very seldom get things right first time. Many courses need to be run up to six times before being anywhere near fully-debugged. It is always sensible — and professional — to explicitly designate the first occurrence as a pilot course.

Handling questions

The prepared part of your lecture is what is under your control. It is the comments, suggestions and questions from the audience that are less predictable. Yet these are the most important part of most teaching. Students can always read the content of our lectures; understanding and acceptance comes from applying what we are teaching. Frequently this takes the form of asking for further explanation or for how the theory being expounded fits a given set of circumstances within a student's own environment.

Suppose you have been listening to a lecturer explaining inflation accounting, quality circles or desktop publishing. You ask a question. He fails to answer it. Very quickly the lecturer loses all credibility. We invariably judge lecturers by their ability to answer questions. As Lewis Carroll pointed out, when a clock strikes 13 you do not just disbelieve the last strike; it throws doubt on everything that has gone before. Similarly, a lecturer unable to answer questions loses credibility over all that he says. Conversely, handling questions with assurance and ease imparts confidence in the complete message. That is why the only acceptable method of handling questions is to know the answer. Consistent failure to know the answers does not result from the absence of the ability to think on one's feet; it results from inadequacies in preparation. However, none of us is perfect, so if you are caught out here is my hardened-up version of how to get yourself out of trouble. The suggested ploys are in increasing order of desperation.

Admit ignorance

Provided the question is not one to which you clearly should have an answer, admission of ignorance is an acceptable, and often effective, technique. Come clean, but promise to find out — and then make sure you do. Even so there are many ways of admitting ignorance. Only the novice will concede: 'I really haven't the foggiest'. More experienced lecturers will choose a form of words that implies a certain knowledge though not precisely what the questioner wants: 'It's difficult to give a precise answer in this context'. Notice that 'precise' implies he could give a rough answer but prefers not to do so; 'in this context' equally conveys the impression of an available answer but one which the presenter (being a perfectionist) prefers not to reveal because it is not directly related to the questioner's own environment.

"I'm pleased you asked me that..."

Defer the answer

'Can I get back to you on that one?' Or safer (since it is always dangerous to give the questioner an option — he might reply 'No, I'd like the answer now'): 'I'd like to come back to you'. You then hope that the questioner forgets or that you have time to discover the answer. A variation of this is:

Drop someone else in it.

This can only be done where you are team teaching. A difficult question can then be deflected with the comment: 'My colleague will be dealing with that later'. Note the use of the word 'colleague'; 'friend' is inappropriate in this context. If he was one up till then, he will not be thereafter.

169

Get the audience to answer it

This is a variation of the above, to be used when you do not have any other co-presenter to get you out of it. Without being too obvious about it you rely on someone in your audience to come up with the answer: 'Jane, I thought you might like to come in on this one'. This, of course, presupposes some earlier identification of Jane as knowing something about the subject, but this is merely prudent data gathering.

Answer a different question.

This can be done overtly or covertly. Overtly you thank the person for the question and rephrase it into something to which you do know the answer: 'I think what you're really asking is . . .'. Done covertly means answering a different question without admitting it. This is the commonest method of politicians. Note how, when asked, 'What real chance do you think there is of this legislation being passed?', their reply begins 'I fervently hope that . . .'. We know what they hope. The actual question asked was what they thought of their chances.

Whether done overtly or covertly, it is imperative that you avoid eye contact with the questioner. If possible, take another question from elsewhere in the audience; then it will appear rude if the original questioner interrupts to say you have not answered his question. Needless to say, on no account must you ask: 'Have I answered your question?'

Outlaw the question

An advanced version of answering a different question comes from Margaret Thatcher. Faced with an unwanted question she is apt to respond, 'What you should really be asking is . . .'.

But even the British prime minister has to give second best to the former premier of Queensland, Sir Joh Bjelke Petersen. Confronted with awkward policy questions from journalists or electors his stock response was: 'Don't you worry yourself about that'. If only we mere lecturers had the courage to emulate that!

References

1. Herzberg, Frederick; Mousner, Bernard and Bloch Sayderman, Barbara; *The Motivation to Work*; second edition; John Wiley & Sons; 1959.
2. Rosenthal, R. Professor of Social Psychology, Harvard.

14
Common presentational problems

In the course of my own career in training I must have lectured to well over five thousand students and listened to around three hundred presentations. I am therefore strongly aware of the presentational faults that occur in teaching. The following — divided into problems in the presenter and problems in the audience — are the most common. Most presenter faults are hard and can be cured by practice (once you are aware that you have them); audience problems, though falling into the general categories listed below, are caused by other people. They are therefore never exactly the same from one course to the next. Since dealing with people is, by definition, person-dependent you may go about it a different way from the way I do. You must in consequence take the advice proffered as suggestions rather than rules.

The presenter's

Nerves
Knowledge of your material is a greater aid to overcoming nerves than any amount of widely-recommended deep-breathing exercises. In any case, a certain degree of nervousness is an essential stimulant. Familiarity should breed fluency, not contempt. The opposite of extreme nervousness is not confidence — it is over-confidence. And over-confidence usually comes before a fall. If you treat each course you give as different from any you have given before (it is, because you have a different audience), you should feel some twinge of apprehension that everything will go as planned. If you feel no nervousness, the danger light should come on because you are probably getting blasé about what you are teaching, having done the same course so many times before.

Nevertheless, there is a distinct difference between healthy nervousness and blank terror. Excessive nervousness mostly arises from the fear

.... There is a difference between healthy
nervousness and blank terror.

that you will be made to look stupid, which in turn arises from being
floored by a question. If I am lecturing near my level of competence, my
body language and delivery inhibit questions; all the while I have plenty
in hand, I am doing all I can to encourage them.

Take heart. Whatever embarrassment you may suffer, someone has
gone one better. I was watching a performance of Beethoven's Ninth
Symphony at the London Barbican. In front of the four principal singers
was an audience of two thousand; behind them were the massed ranks
of the London Symphony Orchestra and Chorus. The bass soloist rose
and started to sing. He was motioned to sit down by the conductor. He
had come in three minutes too early.

Screen-gazing

Probably the commonest of all lecturer faults is not looking at the
audience. This most frequently takes the form of staring fixedly at your
own visuals. When you are explaining a diagram or table to an audience
it is essential to maintain eye contact. This gives the audience the chance
to ask questions and enables the lecturer to observe body language and
get feedback. The use of OHP slides means that the presenter can point

172

to the slide on the projector in front of him and thereby maintain his stance towards the class.

A variant of this habit is directing your gaze at one particular person or, more commonly, one side of the lecture room.

Blocking the screen

In setting up the lecture room, the presenter should pay special attention to sight lines to the screen. If you are lucky the screen may be high enough for there to be no problem with the projector itself, or the lecturer, getting in the way. Failing this, the seating may have to be arranged to maximize sight lines, and to ensure the lecturer does not get between projector and screen, or audience and screen, with his body. If he is not careful, he will throw shadows on to the screen and give a magic lantern show instead of a presentation.

A common beginner's mistake is to leave the projector turned on between slides. If there is no gap between one slide and the next it is distracting to turn the projector on and off; but otherwise you should never leave a screen illuminated without a visual on it. If you are worried about blowing the bulb or distracting your audience, by frequent turning on and off, use a cardboard cover over the light source.

A magic lantern show

Note-reading

If ever I listen to a presenter who is a total slave to his notes I feel like saying 'Why not give us your notes to read and let's get on with the lesson?'. Notes should be an *aide-mémoire*, not a detailed narrative of everything you intend to say. If you do need to refer to notes, arrange to place them high enough so that you reduce the angle between consulting your notes and looking at your audience. This will minimize the loss of eye contact. Your visuals should serve the function of your major notes; all that you then need to recall is the commentary you give on each. After running the session a couple of times, this should become easier.

Conducting the audience

One way of not obscuring what is on the screen is to point at it with a baton. Beware! These are dangerous instruments in the hands of presenters. For a start, they are apt to make people feel self-important. There is something of the schoolmaster's cane about a pointer and I always suffer from an uncontrollable urge to rap someone across the knuckles with it if they are not attending. Secondly, there is the ever-lurking danger of waving it as though one were conducting an orchestra or using it as a back-scratcher. Other common problems that presenters have with their hands include emphasizing a point with a devastating left hook, jingling coins in pockets, scratching various parts of their anatomy, and stuffing fingers up the ends of marker pens.

..... scratching various parts of one's anatomy
and stuffing fingers up the ends of marker pens.

Voice-dropping

If the lecturer does not sound enthusiastic about the topic, what chance
does the student have? Tape your talk in private and listen to yourself.
Check that you do not drop your voice at the end of sentences. This is
the quickest way of sending people to sleep. If you sound slow and flat
make an effort to speed up and put a spring in your voice. Keep your
audience on their toes. Ask questions, rather than declaim truths, even
if the questions are rhetorical. Your intonation for asking questions is
different from that when making statements and this will help to vary
your delivery. Refer to individuals by name if asking actual questions.
This not only involves that person, it makes other people think that their
turn is coming.

Personal mannerisms

Most of us have some mannerisms that can grate over a period of time.
These can vary from verbal habits such as 'ums and ahs' or 'you know'
repeated frequently, to coin tossing, pacing up and down like a caged
tiger, earlobe-pulling or finger-nail biting.

First you have to find out whether you have such a mannerism — most
are completely unconscious. A quality review of one of your presentations will soon uncover them. Initially, becoming conscious of them only
makes it worse. In time, practice will enable you to eliminate the worst.

"Unaccustomed as I am to standing still....."

The audience

No course is complete without someone whose only apparent reason for coming is to make your life a misery. The way in which a lecturer handles problem members of an audience is very personal. Some people confront them directly, others prefer to use humour to defuse the situation. Yet others ignore them, soldiering on in the hope that things can only get better. Below is a list of the most common troublemakers with suggestions on how to deal with them.

The snoozer

The danger time is just after lunch (known in lecturing circles as the graveyard shift), caused by too great an intake of food and drink during the break period. The most entertaining speaker will have problems with someone with two large gins and a three-course meal inside him. The most important point to make is that if someone begins to drop off in your class it is already too late to do much about it. Snoozing is a problem encountered during the presentation phase but usually caused by insufficient thought at the specification or design stage. We should therefore address the possibility of this problem during these stages. This gives us two useful rules:

1. Keep lunches light and serve no alcohol.
2. Arrange the course timetable so that there is a participative session immediately after lunch.

The Snoozer

Attention to these two simple rules should minimize the chance of people snoozing. However, if despite this somebody is showing distinct signs of nodding-off, you can dynamically select one of the following techniques — depending on who he is (don't throw water over the managing director), and the urgency of the situation:

1. Unless his drooping head is distracting other members of the audience, if you are close to the end of the session, or until such time as his snoring grows so loud as to drown your speaking voice or wake other people, it may be prudent to ignore him. Statistically, this coward's route is the most common — including my own courses.

2. Throw a question at him. If your objective is merely to wake him (rather than to draw attention to his behaviour) then you should word your question carefully so as to avoid embarrassment:

   - Start with the person's name so that he has a chance to wake up in time to hear the body of the question.
   - Phrase the question in such a way that even if he only wakes up half-way through he can still make an appropriate response: 'Peter, that is how we draw this diagram, isn't it?'

3. More subtle, address a question to the person next to him. The

177

change in the direction from which sound is coming when the question is answered should be sufficient to bring him back to life.

4. Pour a jug of water over him. This will make you the hero of your class. However, it is likely to entail adverse side-effects and I cannot be held responsible for anything that may happen to you as a result of following this advice.

The reader

"......But on page 101 you say........"

This is the person that ignores what you are saying whilst he browses through the manual (thereby seeing in advance all your spontaneous jokes). The simplest solution is to deprive him of anything to read. Distribute sections of the manual only as they arise or at the end of the session. If you prefer to give out the manual at the start of the course make it clear in your introduction that the manual acts as a back-up and should not be read in advance.

The over-qualified

The over-qualified person should not really be on the course. He is much more knowledgeable than the other participants. If students introduce themselves at the beginning of the course then it is likely to be obvious to everyone. There is thus no advantage to be gained from pretending it has not happened. Deal with it straight away: 'Well, Jim, you obviously are already familiar with much of what I am going to be saying in the first few sessions. You will just have to sit back and admire the beauty of the exposition. Please don't wince more than necessary.' The latter comment is because the most frequent occurrence of this for me is the computer manager who decides to sit in on a course I am giving for his senior management. I know that in teaching hard/soft to my audience I shall be oversimplifying many complex computer matters. As we have seen, one cannot do this without some element of distortion.

Another tactic is to invoke Bolden's rule (see p. 167) by using the enlistment technique: 'Actually I'm very pleased that you are on the course [lying is a technique not much covered in books], because you will be able to help me refer the general principles to your specific systems'. This can be done openly or at a break: 'I'm glad you've been able to come along [once you get into lying mode it is difficult to get out of it] I always think it important that the manager show his commitment. I've got a hands-on session after lunch. Do you think you could give me a hand. You know what it's like with people that haven't used computers before.'

The wise guy

"I think you mean uninterested rather than disinterested....."

The wise guy is more interested in impressing other members of the audience with his brilliance or wisdom than in listening to what you have to say. How you deal with him is largely a matter of his position within the company and your own self-confidence. If he is the managing director then you will have to put up with his remarks; if he is a subordinate showing-off in front of his superiors, it is quite likely that someone in the audience will lose patience and deal with him for you. The best strategy is to allow him enough rope to hang himself. Tell yourself that leopards do not change their spots — he may be making your life miserable for three days, but his colleagues have him for the rest of the year. Remain excessively polite and helpful. As long as you obey this rule the rest of the audience will be on your side and you will come out looking better than he does. When he asks a question or makes a comment treat it as a serious one, answer as best you can and keep going. There is a golden rule here: if you lose patience, or let your irritation show, you have lost the battle — Don't get mad, get even. Bide your time. You may find a better opportunity later in the week, by which time you have got to know the other participants better. There are many more effective ways of dealing with the wise guy than taking him on in class.

Postscript:
the ten truths of teaching

One of the classic communication sequences is:

- 'Tell 'em what you are going to tell 'em
- Tell 'em
- Then tell 'em what you've told 'em.'

This leads authors and presenters towards a summary of the main teaching points. Since this book expressly advocates hardening up soft subjects by devising rules, or if not rules then guidelines, it is appropriate to conclude with the ten truths of teaching. (By now I trust that you are sufficiently cynical to see that 'ten' is chosen for alliteration rather than illumination.)

1. Follow a clear method for course development that enforces consultation and technical reviews of defined deliverables.
2. Concentrate on getting the specification right. Without this, much design and writing effort will be wasted.
3. Be sensitive to individuals' different learning styles.
4. Get a good course structure — allocation of time and determination of sequence.
5. Design a course that uses a variety of training methods and aids.
6. Make sure that you understand the course material before trying to impart understanding to others.
7. Take a pride in your writing — both words and visuals.
8. Be aware of your own teaching style and improve those areas in which you are weakest.
9. Regard all courses as a learning opportunity for yourself.
10. Make learning stimulating and enjoyable. You have students in front of you for only a very low proportion of the time in which they will apply what you have taught. The greatest service any teacher can perform is to make a subject come alive. If you succeed in doing this your students will go on learning long after they have left your course.

Bibliography

General
Approaches to Training and Development, 2nd ed., Gavin Laird, Addison-Wesley, 1985
How to Communicate 2nd ed., Gordon Wells, McGraw Hill, 1986
Managing the Training and Development Function, Allan Pepper, Gower, 1984
Manual of Learning Styles, Peter Honey and Alan Mumford, Peter Honey, Maidenhead 1982
Producing Workshops, Seminars and Short Courses: A Trainer's Handbook, John W. Loughary and Barry Hopson, Follett, 1979
The Skills of Communicating, Bill Scott, Gower, 1986
The Skills of Training, Leslie Rae, Gower, 1983
Train The Trainer, Michael Birkenbihl, Chartwell Bratt, 1983
Using Your Learning Styles, Peter Honey and Alan Mumford, Peter Honey, Maidenhead 1983

Specification
Preparing Instructional Objectives, 2nd ed., Robert S. Mager, Belmont CA, Fearon, 1975
Taxonomy of Educational Objectives, B.S. Bloom McKay, 1956

Design
Computer-based Training, Greg Kearsley, Addison Wesley, 1983
Producing Workshops, Seminars and Short courses: A Trainer's Handbook, John W. Loughary and Barry Hopson, Follett, 1979

Writing
Case Studies in Systems Analysis, John Race, Macmillan, 1979
Drawing on the Right Side of the Brain, Betty Edwards, Fontana, 1982
Games Trainers Play, John Newstrom and Edward Scannell, McGraw Hill, 1980
Slide Rules, Antony Jay, Video Arts, 1976
The Brain Book, Peter Russell, Routledge and Kegan Paul, 1979
The Economist Pocket Style Book, Economist Publications, 1986
Using your Overhead Projector, Chris Waller, Fordigraph, 1983
Your Memory — A User's Guide, Alan Baddeley, Pelican, 1983

Presentation
Body Language, Allan Pease, Camel Publishing, 1981

Effective Speaking and Presentation for the Company Executive, Clive T. Goodworth, Business Books, 1980

Know What I Mean?, G.A. Lord, McGraw-Hill, 1978

Presenting a Training Session, Manpower Services Commission, 1985

Reaching Out: Interpersonal Effectiveness and Self-Actualisation, D.W. Johnson, Prentice Hall, 1987

Evaluation

Evaluation of Management Education, Training and Development, Mark Easterby-Smith, Gower, 1986

Index